Universal Messages

Universal Messages
A Guidebook For The Expanding Human

by

Elizabeth McConahay Wanfried

Dedication

This book is dedicated to me and my fellow humans who are growing, expanding and evolving along with Mother Earth and our vast Universe itself.

To anyone who feels their soul's awakening and the indescribable pulse of universal energy, this book is for you.

If you find yourself here, on the opening pages of this little book, you are exactly where you are supposed to be. This is your moment. This is your book.

Take from it what you will, leave behind anything that's not for you.

My energetic imprint is on each page of this offering. I infused this book with love, my highest hopes for all who read it, and my own perfect imperfections.

With Love From Liz,
May, 2017

How To Use This Book

This is your book now, and you can and should use it any way you like! But let me tell you a bit about why I structured it the way I did, and share some possible approaches you might take.

I chose to include 52 Messages in this volume because throughout my own work with the messages (which I receive and publish daily through www.WithLoveFromLiz.com), I always find myself wishing that I had more time to spend with each Message.

So for that reason I chose 52 Messages for this book, in case you, like me, might want to read one message per week and have the rest of the week to work with it before receiving the next one. It's a quite nice way to deep dive into the ideas, and even cultivate behavioral changes around them if you so choose.

Or, here's another approach. Throughout my life, I have had my own intuitive "way" of using books— and that has been to open up to any page of whatever book is at hand, and interpret its divine meaning for me on the spot.

Sometimes I hear the number of a certain page called in my mind, and I open the book accordingly, which, in the case of this book here, you could do for yourself by choosing a Message number to open up to, whenever you feel like it!

Whatever way you choose will be just perfect for you.

I have also had the experience with the Messages that, just like with any oracle one might use, the interpretation of the Message is completely different depending on when you're working with it, and under what circumstances! So, no matter how many times I revisit a Message, each day (moment!) brings with it an opportunity to feel its resonance in a new and perhaps deeper way.

Now, a note about my "notes"…

When I published these daily Messages to my subscribers each morning, I often included my own "take" on the day's Message, and there's an important reason why I did this!

First of all, please remember, that these Messages are for ME as well as you! The wisdom contained in the Universal Messages began as answers to my own heartfelt questions. And the guidance that comes through continues to blow my mind daily in the most beautiful ways! I need this guidance too, just like you.

Also, I have included my responses in this volume as a way for you to potentially see the Messages from another angle, if you will. We each have our own interpretation of everything we read or hear, and sometimes bearing witness to another's experience with the same material can help our personal expansion exponentially!

I would recommend that you read each original message for yourself, and let it resonate as it will. From there, you might even document your impressions of the message in a notebook or journal, for reference. If you choose to read my notes on the Message as well and they are useful to you, fantastic!

Where Are The Universal Messages Coming From?

In 2015, my spiritual journey took a decided turn toward expansion. For the first time in my life, I had gotten consistent with my meditation practice, and the space that that created in my life allowed some pretty significant (to me) experiences of awareness to flow in.

My perceptions of light, sound, vibration… all changed and heightened, and even the experience of what it felt like to dwell inside my own physical body was upended!

I now see sunlight in a new way with individual rays discernible from one another, a *white instead of *golden quality to the light, and fully articulated rainbow spectrums within each one. I hear frequencies and tones in communicative patterns, and I communicate completely differently with Earth's creatures (insects, plants, bodies of water, etc.)

But one of the most fascinating changes in my awareness came through my journal. I had begun to keep copious notes on my energetic experiences, as each day brought about shifts that were so brand new to me and so multi-faceted… I wanted to be sure I chronicled all of them!

As events progressed, I began to ask questions, sort of "out loud" in my journal. I wanted to know more about what I was going through, and why! And this is where I experienced the most profound element of my journey yet: I got answers, immediately.

As soon as I would write a question, and sometimes before I had even written out all of the words, I HEARD the answer coming through my ears loud and clear and FAST, and my pen would struggle to keep up to write it down! These messages came through (and still do) in ALL CAPITAL LETTERS and in a distinctive tone that feels comforting and profoundly wise all at once.

This phenomenon has continued ever since. Every time I ask a question or even enter into a state of openness to serve, the guidance comes pouring through. Always fast. Always in capital letters. Always in its own unique voice.

As of this writing, hundreds of messages have come through. Sometimes I ask a specific question and receive a specific answer. Sometimes I open myself up and ask for what wants to come through for the greatest good. No matter how I request it, the information comes faithfully flowing through.

Initially I wondered *where* the messages were coming from. Were they coming from Me? From God? Source, Spirit, a Guardian Angel, Outer Space?

I knew one thing. The messages weren't coming through my conscious awareness. The reason I knew this was because, for one thing, I "heard" the messages, and also, they came through in one uninterrupted stream, no pauses or breaks.

I know that when I, "Conscious Liz," sit down to do writing of my own, the words take time in coming. I edit, I ponder, I rearrange, until what I want to say feels right and clear to me. But with the Messages, there is no need to edit, everything comes pouring through, and all I need to do is insert a few paragraph spaces for my readers afterward, just to break up the run-on sentence of flow.

Another distinction between my "own" writing and the Messages is the cadence and vernacular used in the Messages. When they come through, the tone is decidedly more declarative than my own writing voice, more authoritative, and yet loving. My own written cadence is more casual and meandering.

But the biggest insight I got into the "where are these coming from?" question came during one of my writing sessions where I asked deliberately what my role was in all this. I wrote the question into my book, and immediately the answer came pouring through as always, but *this time* it included a phrase I had never heard of before. I had to stop and look it up on line!

It was then that I realized that even though the messages come "through" me, there is a higher (or I prefer the idea of *more expanded*) energy at their origin— a consciousness that has access to a vocabulary I myself don't yet possess!

And now, after transcribing hundreds of these Messages, I know that I am accessing them through my own unique expression of the Great Creation. That's a term I coined for my own experience of what some might call God, Source, Spirit, etc, and I use many of those terms interchangeably with my own.

But to me this Great Creation is all around us *and* within us! It is our Earth, our Bodies, Our Universe, and beyond. We have access to more of the Great Creation when we ask for it, and when we make space in our lives to hear its wisdom. Does it come from within me? Yes. Does it come from outside of me? Yes and no, because nothing is outside of me. We are all facets, beautiful individual facets, of this epic Great Creation.

The expression of our own unique facet is whatever we are currently allowing it to be, but we are never fully expressed! And that is exactly why these messages are coming through— to help us expand into more and more expressions of our unique selves/essences!

So the reason I call this guidance The Universal Messages is twofold: First, I know that it does *come from* the Universe. The Divine Energetic Universe that is and encompasses all of you and me. Secondly, the messages themselves are *universal* in nature.

After a few months of the Messages coming through me and into my own private journal, I shared some of the excerpts with a few dear friends. Without exception, my friends responded that the timing of the messages (though intended, I thought, for myself) hit home with them in really personal and uncanny ways!

Not long afterward, the Messages began to tell me that I was supposed to be sharing this guidance. I was pretty reticent at first. This type of interface with Great Creation was new to me, and I had no idea how I would be regarded if I brought these Messages forward, or even how I would do it! But as the Messages stayed consistent, my comfort level with this communication grew, and eventually I knew and really believed that it was indeed my mission to share what I was receiving. I knew that as the timing was right, the way to do this would be shown to me, and I was right.

Now the Messages are shared via a free e-mail every weekday morning to my subscribers around the world, and this first book has been born! Who knew? (Obviously The Universe!)

My readers' letters to me echo stories of how the Messages help them during times of personal transformation, during life transitions ranging from career changes to grieving departed loved ones, and how the perspective shifts suggested in The Messages help them shift from complacency into joy!

I pray and know that the Messages will find their way into your experience at precisely the right time and in the most helpful way for you. As the Messenger, I could ask for no greater gift than to be serving in this way.

THE MESSAGES

Message 1:
Expansion

OPEN UP YOUR MIND AND GET RID OF
IT BASICALLY. PULL IT APART UNTIL IT
LETS THE SUN SHINE IN. BE WILLING
TO BREAK THE FIBERS, THAT THEY
MIGHT GROW BACK IN NEW,
HEALTHIER PATTERNS. SEE THE
PATHWAYS NOW THAT NEVER SAW
THE LIGHT OF DAY. NOTICE THAT
THERE ARE NO STREET SIGNS AND NO
MAP ON THIS JOURNEY. JUST YOUR
OWN SINGULAR AND UNIQUE URGE
TO _MOVE_ IN THE DIRECTION OF YOUR
SOUL'S EXPANSION.

Ah, the voice of Spirit minces no words! I do
love the graphic imagery of physically breaking
our own restrictive fibers. Months after I

transcribed this message, I discovered the technique of myofascial release through an amazing practitioner named Nicole Rainerman. To my amazement, this "fiber-breaking" technique is something I was able to learn and implement in ways that would free up motion in my physical body that had been restricted for years!

So now I have a beautiful go-to experience to use when I start thinking about "pulling apart" the fibers of my mind and letting them regrow healthily. Consequently I feel freer across the board now— mentally, emotionally, physically.

MESSAGE 2:
Awareness

OVER YOUR LIFE YOU EXPERIENCE
TALL TREES, SUNSETS, MOONBEAMS…
WITHOUT EVEN STOPPING TO TUNE
IN TO WHAT THOSE THINGS ARE.
WHAT'S GOING ON THERE? BE STILL
WITH JUST ONE THING YOU TAKE FOR
GRANTED AND YOU'LL OVERCOME
YOUR ENERGETIC STAGNATION. THIS
AWARENESS IS THE KEY TO THE
FORWARD MOTION YOU SEEK.

I'm really enjoying the literal interpretation we can take with the opening words: "Over your life..." suggesting not just "over" the course of our lives, but asking us to understand that all of these phenomena are taking place OVER us! Look up!

And the irony of being HUMANS who long for that sense of progress and accomplishment, yet we miss so many moments for truly epic contemplation!

Whether it's the cosmos or the person right in front of us... what are we taking for granted? What questions have we forgotten to ask, like: "How long can we stay in this planetary orbit?" or even just: "How are you doing, friend?"

Message 3:
Relationships are Barometers

YOUR RELATIONSHIPS ARE YOUR
BAROMETER FOR YOUR LEVEL OF
EARTHLY CONNECTION. WHEN YOU
CONNECT TO EARTH AND GENERATE
THAT CONNECTION UP AND INTO
YOUR BODY AND THEN INTO YOUR
RELATIONSHIPS, YOU ARE
COMPLETING A CIRCUIT OF LOVE.

SOME WOULD CALL THIS
"GROUNDEDNESS," BUT REALLY
GROUNDING IS ALSO LOVE. JUST
EXPAND YOUR DEFINITION.

THE WAY THIS PLAYS OUT IN YOUR
RELATIONSHIPS IS THAT, QUITE

LITERALLY, IF YOU HAVE GROUNDED YOUR ELECTRICAL CHARGE INTO EARTH, YOU SIMPLY HAVE DIFFERENT QUALITIES OF CONVERSATIONS AND REACTIONS. PLAY WITH THIS.

I'm re-reading this message, trying to pull from it everything it has to offer. It's not JUST reminding me to ground myself (a reminder I've really needed as I feel myself taking in more and more energy lately) but it takes us one step further into how our relationships are showing up and why.

I don't usually think of grounding in terms of my relationships, do you? This is opening a door for me for sure. We're being asked to "play with this" so what does that mean?

For me, first I think I'll explore taking extra steps to ground myself in general (a/k/a LOTS more time outdoors), and then for the "play with this" part, I'm going to make an effort to ground myself into Earth either before or during my conversations with others. (Maybe even AFTER, if necessary!)

Message 4:
Breathe From The Soul

BREATHE FROM THE SOUL.

WHAT DOES THAT MEAN?

INTAKE MORE THAN YOU EVER
THOUGHT YOU COULD WITH EACH
INHALATION. AS THOUGH YOUR
LUNGS ARE INFINITY SWIMMING
POOLS AND YOUR EFFORT OF BREATH
DRAWS IN PLACID RIPPLES ACROSS
THEIR SURFACES.

IF YOU CONNECT THE "SOUL'S
BREATH" TO YOUR DAILY TASKS,
YOU'RE TAKING IN A BREATH THAT
WILL FORTIFY ALL THAT YOU DO

WITH WHO YOU ARE. AND AS YOU
EXHALE, THIS IS THE BREATH OF GOD.

I am grateful for this.
I feel like this Soul's Breath exercise is bringing
me back to myself, safely home.

We get plenty of reminders these days to
breathe. And that's a good thing. I think a lot
of suffering could be avoided just by engaging
in a little more breathing.

But this idea... the Soul's Breath... feels so
comforting to me. I tried it. It truly goes
outside of the moment we're in, and comes
back to the moment we're in. In one beautiful,
limitless cycle.

I notice it doesn't specify to take in "air." It asks
us to take in "more than we ever thought we

could." What does that mean for you? For me, it lets me know that there's so much more to draw upon than we could even wrap our minds around. Yet when we just surf the wave of our breath as far as we can ride it, we reach ourselves, which is what then "fortifies what we do with who we are"....

And that is the Breath of God.

That I believe.

It's all about the cycles. Learning, learning, knowing, growing.

XO, Liz

Message 5:
Your Vessel

BECOME A VESSEL. AN EMPTY VESSEL.
YOU CAN ENVISION THIS BY SIMPLY
TAKING A BREATH OR TWO TO
"CLEAN OUT YOUR INSIDES" AND A
BIG SHOULDER SHRUG AND RELEASE
TO "DROP AWAY" ANYTHING THAT
FEELS STUCK TO YOU.

NOW. NOW THAT YOU'RE AN EMPTY
VESSEL, WHAT WANTS TO HAPPEN? A-
HA! THINGS WANT TO COME IN AND
FILL YOU UP AGAIN!

BUT WAIT! WE'RE GOING TO DO TWO
QUICK STEPS HERE.

FIRST. STAY EMPTY. FOR AS LONG AS YOU CAN. KEEP THE DEEP BREATHS GOING, SHRUG AND RELEASE AS MANY TIMES AS YOU NEED TO, AND TRY TO STAY EMPTY. FOR A FEW BREATHS OR A FEW MINUTES, WHATEVER YOU CAN MANAGE.

NOW. WHAT IS WANTING TO COME IN AND FILL YOUR VESSEL? THOUGHTS? EMOTIONS? WORRIES? COMPLAINTS? PHYSICAL SENSATIONS? OTHERS' NEEDS?

WHAT ARE THESE THINGS THAT SO DESPERATELY RUSH TO FILL THAT SPACE? TAKE NOTE OF THEM, IF YOU CAN.

NOW PAUSE AND REMIND YOURSELF: IT'S YOUR CHOICE. IT'S YOUR CHOICE WHAT YOU ALLOW TO FILL YOUR VESSEL AND TAKE UP RESIDENCE IN YOUR BODY AND MIND.

TIME TO BE A BETTER GATEKEEPER. YOU DECIDE WHAT COMES IN, WHAT GOES OUT. CURATE THE CONTENTS OF YOUR VESSEL WISELY AND GENTLY. TAKE NOTE OF WHAT YOU WANT YOUR INSIDES TO LOOK LIKE, AND WHAT IS STUCK IN YOU THAT NEEDS TO BE LOVINGLY ESCORTED OUT.

HOW LIFE SHOWS UP FOR YOU ON THE OUTSIDE WILL HAVE EVERYTHING TO DO WITH HOW WELL YOU TEND THE

GARDEN OF YOUR HEART. USE YOUR VESSEL WISELY. IT IS CAPABLE OF MORE THAN YOU KNOW RIGHT NOW.

This is one I really take to heart every single day. I began this process of tending to my vessel a few years ago by "curating" my Facebook feed. Even though I was only connected on Facebook to people I *actually know and am friends with*, I still found I needed to limit my exposure to what I was allowing their posts to "feed" me every day.

Eventually I found that the best fit for me was to not engage with social media at all for several months. But there are other sources of accidental exposure to vessel pollution that we can really train ourselves to limit or do away with. The nightly news (or news feeds) is certainly one of them, and all it takes to stop seeing or hearing it is simply not turning it on.

But the more subtle and unavoidable toxic intruders come in the form of daily communication with others who, innocently but habitually, choose to engage by way of low vibrational conversations. Tuning into the subject matter and asking ourselves if this information serves us or our relationships takes a bit of adjustment, but once you "set your dial" to engaging in and receiving high quality communication, you'll soon hardly be able to tolerate anything else! And that's a good thing, because it begins to attract to you more and more high-quality relationships!

Part of setting your dial might include addressing others' communication choices, and for the non-confrontational among us, this can be tricky. But if you struggle with that part, re-read the message above. You are the sole gatekeeper of your vessel. If you don't tend to its contents, no one will.

The way I've dealt with people in my life who are chronic complainers, or who tend to gravitate toward gossip, sensationalistic news, or other low-vibrational content as source material for conversation, is by letting them know that my tolerance for that type of content is low. This way I keep the focus on my preferences and needs, as opposed to criticizing them for reaching for low-hanging-fruit, as it were.

And remember, people don't even realize they're doing it! In fact, you might be a culprit yourself! But when we ask of ourselves or others: *Why am I telling this story? Why are you sharing this with me?* we soon realize that it's not fair to bring conversational pollution to others, and it's not fair for others to bring it to us!

I know now from personal experience that cleaning up our acts in this way is one of the fastest routes to joy.

Sending love!
XO, Liz

Message 6:
Our Animal Teachers

WE CAN ABSORB SO MUCH VALUABLE WISDOM FROM OUR FELLOW BEINGS IN THE ANIMAL WORLD, BUT FIRST IT IS NECESSARY TO HONOR THEIR COMMUNICATION STYLES. DON'T PERSONALIZE THEIR GESTURES, BUT INSTEAD LOOK INTO THE NECESSITY OF THEIR ACTIONS.

WHAT IS THE TAKEAWAY WHEN WE DON'T INTERPRET THE CREATURES' ACTIONS THROUGH THE SAME PARAMETERS WITH WHICH WE WOULD ASSESS OUR OWN?

WHAT CAN BE LEARNED FROM THE PROXIMITY OF THE ANIMALS TO THEIR YOUNG, FOR EXAMPLE? WHAT PURPOSE IS BEING SERVED THERE?

STAY WITH THE IDEA OF PURPOSE, NOT PERSONALITY WHEN YOU ARE LEANING TOWARD THE ANIMALS FOR

WISDOM, AND THE INSIGHTS WILL
APPEAR.

HOW DOES A CAT INTEGRATE
CONFLICT? HOW DOES
SHE PHYSICALLY RELEASE THE
CONFLICT ENERGY AFTERWARD? HOW
DOES A SKUNK FUNCTION
UNTHREATENED IN HIS
ENVIRONMENT--WHAT ROLE DOES HIS
DEFENSE MECHANISM PLAY IN
RELATION TO HIS FEARS?

LINE UP THE TRAITS OF THESE
BEAUTIFUL CREATURES WITH YOUR
OWN STRUGGLES AND TRIALS. HOW
ARE THE ANIMALS BUILT TO COPE?
WHAT HABITS ARE THE UNIQUE
COPING SKILLS OF THE ANIMALS
AROUND YOU MODELING?

I'm so glad we're being called to tune into inter-
species wisdom. The directive here takes me
out of some of my old interpretive habits and
asks me to implement new ones. This concept
of honoring the animals' behavior as functional,

purposeful, and inherently wise is one I can't wait to work with. I really think this opens up the field of animal energy to help us find wisdom through tuning into whatever animals or animal images are at hand, instead of patently categorizing animals based on just their symbolic associations.

What a beautiful new approach to tuning in.

Sending love today, as ever!
XO, Liz

Message 7:
If You Think You Can't Create Your Reality,
You're Right

YOU HAVE THE ABILITY TO MAKE ALL THE CHOICES IN YOUR REALITY. THE FACT THAT YOU DON'T AGREE WITH THAT STATEMENT IS EXACTLY WHAT'S KEEPING IT FROM BEING TRUE FOR YOU.

YOUR REALITY IS SELF IMPOSED. THESE STATEMENTS AREN'T POPULAR, WHICH IS WHY YOUR PATTERNS FEEL SO INESCAPABLE.

HOW CAN YOU SUSPEND YOUR DISBELIEF, TRULY? HOW, AFTER A LIFETIME OF SELF-LIMITING BELIEFS, CAN YOU MAKE A SHIFT IN YOUR REALITY?

HERE IS A KEY:

GO INTO A TASK WITH NO DISTRACTIONS. FEEL EVERY SENSATION AND LOOK FOR THE NEW ONES THAT YOU HAVEN'T ALLOWED YOURSELF TO TAKE NOTICE OF BEFORE.

YOU MUST TRAIN YOURSELF TO BE ABLE TO IMMERSE YOURSELF IN AN EXPERIENCE SO THOROUGHLY THAT NOTHING ELSE CROSSES YOUR MIND AND INTERFERES.

WHAT'S THE MOST IMMERSIVE EXPERIENCE YOU CURRENTLY DO? PAINTING? WALKING IN NATURE? TAKING A BATH? READING?

START WITH THE MOST IMMERSIVE EXPERIENCE YOU CURRENTLY DO, WHATEVER YOU GET THE MOST LOST IN, WHATEVER MAKES YOU COMPLETELY LOSE TRACK OF TIME.

NOW, CREATE FROM THERE. THAT IMMERSION ENVIRONMENT IS YOUR MOST POWERFUL CREATION POINT RIGHT NOW. BECAUSE IT'S THE PUREST VIBRATION YOU'RE REACHING.

ONCE YOU'RE IMMERSED, YOU'RE GOING TO ASK YOURSELF WHAT ELEMENTS OR REALITY CREATION YOU COULD BRING INTO THAT EXPERIENCE. ADD THEM IN.

FOR EXAMPLE, IF IT'S A BOOK YOU'RE IMMERSED IN, CREATE A DEEPER REALITY IN THE BOOK. ADD DYNAMICS TO THE ATMOSPHERE OF THE STORY THAT EXERCISE YOUR OWN CREATIVE POWER.

TRAIN YOURSELF TO DO THIS WITH YOUR CURRENT IMMERSIVE EXPERIENCES BECAUSE ONCE YOU GET THE HANG OF IT, CO-CREATING YOUR DAILY REALITY WILL TAKE ON A NEW SENSE OF EASE.

USE YOUR GO-TO IMMERSIONS AS YOUR TRAINING GROUND. YOU'VE JUST GOT TO GET OUT OF YOUR OWN WAY AND THAT IS WHERE YOU BEGIN.

I'm so excited about how easy this is to put into practice! Discoveries await us! Have a beautiful day, my friends!
Sending love,
XO Liz

Message 8:
Energetic Communication

YOUR AVENUES OF POTENTIAL
COMMUNICATION ARE NOT BEING
FULLY UTILIZED. THIS IS WHY YOU
FEEL DOUBTFUL ABOUT TELEPATHY,
ENERGY FORMS, THOUGHT FORMS,
ENERGETIC HEALING AND THE LIKE.

YOU SEE-- THE MACHINES YOU USE TO
COMMUNICATE WITH SEEM SO
SOPHISTICATED TO YOU THAT YOU
CAN'T IMAGINE CONVEYING YOUR
MESSAGES IN A LESS PRESCRIPTIVE
WAY.

AND FOR THAT REASON, YOU DO NOT
TRY.

AGAIN, WE MUST LOOK TO NATURE
FOR ITS EXAMPLE OF THE UTMOST IN
ADVANCED INTERPERSONAL
COMMUNICATIONS.

TO GET THE MOST OUT OF YOUR
OBSERVATIONS, YOU'LL NEED TO
WRAP YOUR MIND AROUND THE
CONCEPT OF THE COLLECTIVE.

BECAUSE THE CREATURES OF THIS WORLD ARE OFTEN OPERATING COLLECTIVELY. HENCE, THEY ARE LITERALLY LIGHT YEARS AHEAD OF HUMANS IN TERMS OF COMMUNICATING.

RESEARCH SONAR. OBSERVE FLOCKS OF BIRDS IN FLIGHT. STUDY SCHOOLS OF "LANGUAGE-LESS" FISH, THOUSANDS OF WHICH COORDINATE CHANGES OF DIRECTION INSTANTANEOUSLY AS A GROUP.

THESE WILL NOT BE YOUR PARTICULAR TOOLS FOR COMMUNICATING. BUT THEY WILL BE YOUR EYE OPENING EXAMPLES OF WHAT IS POSSIBLE.

BE WITH THESE ANIMALS IF YOU CAN. FIND A WAY TO OBSERVE THEM AND ALLOW THEIR WISDOM TO SOFTEN YOU. THEN YOU CAN BEGIN TO MOVE FORWARD WITH FINDING YOUR OWN COMMUNICATION PATHWAYS THAT ARE AS YET UNTAPPED BY YOU.

RECONCILE YOUR DOUBTS WITH NATURE'S PROOF FIRST. THE PERFECT ANTIDOTE FOR HUMAN SKEPTICISM.

FROM THERE, ASK YOURSELF TO SHOW YOU WHAT ABILITIES ARE LYING DORMANT. WHEN YOU RECEIVE AN INSIGHT, USE IT IMMEDIATELY. DON'T WAIT. YOU WANT THE RELATIONSHIP BETWEEN YOU AND YOUR HIGHEST ABILITIES TO BE ONE OF TRUST.

This message just cracks me up with its timing. That's because mid-transmission, my computer died, leaving me with nothing but an ominous blinking question mark icon on a blank screen.

As always, I had to lean into this message myself first, and in doing so I didn't allow myself to get frustrated with my technological breakdown. Instead, I tapped into my energy and sat with it, sending it out to all of my subscribers. I sent all the love and energy I was feeling as I thought of each of them.

Then a great friend popped by with her laptop so that I could get this message out for the day, and of course the message and the circumstance all just wove themselves together beautifully.

I always have full faith that precisely what needs to be transmitted will be. And in whatever energetic form is best.

Sending love!
XO, Liz

ROTATING TOWARD THE SUN IS
SOMETHING SO MANY PLANTS AND
ANIMALS DO. THEY ORIENT
THEMSELVES TO OPTIMIZE THE
EFFECTS OF THE SUN ON AND "IN"
THEIR BODIES.

TRY TO ADOPT THIS BEHAVIOR AS
OFTEN AS POSSIBLE, BECAUSE THE
SUN'S BENEFITS ARE SO MUCH
GREATER THAN WHAT YOU'VE BEEN
TAUGHT.

SUN ISN'T JUST AN ENERGY SOURCE.
LOVE COMES FROM THE SUN IN
WAVES. VITAL INFORMATION COMES
INTO US FROM THE SUN. CONSIDER
THE SUN A CHARGING STATION ON
ALL LEVELS FOR YOUR DEPLETED

HUMAN BODY, MIND AND ENERGY
FIELD.

OPEN YOUR MIND TO THIS POINT OF
VIEW AND NOTICE THE FULL
SPECTRUM OF BENEFITS YOU
RECEIVE.

- WHAT NEW INSIGHTS DO YOU
RECEIVE WHEN YOU DELIBERATELY
ENGAGE WITH THE SUN?
- WHAT CREATIVE IDEAS ARE BORN
DURING AND IMMEDIATELY AFTER
YOUR SUN EXPOSURE?
- WHAT EMOTIONAL CHANGES TAKE
PLACE IN YOU WITH DIRECT
SUNLIGHT?
- WHAT NEW KNOWLEDGE DO YOU
POSSESS AFTER A PERIOD OF TIME IN
THE SUN?

IT'S TIME TO HONOR THE MYSTERY
THAT IS THE SUN.

Keep tuning in, guys. Keep going deeper. Keep opening up to the possibilities. Most of what we use as our daily operating system is just what has been told to us, for decades! But what do YOU really know *yourself*?

Have a beautiful day...
Sending love!
XO Liz

Message 10:
It's Not You, It's Me

THERE'S ALL THIS TALK ABOUT
SHIELDING YOURSELF FROM ENERGY
OR "PROTECTING YOURSELF," YOUR
ENERGETIC FIELD, IN SOME WAY.

SOME OF YOU DO GENUINELY TAKE
ON THE VIBRATIONS OF FOLKS
AROUND YOU. THIS CAN BE FELT AS
SUDDEN MOOD SHIFTS OR EVEN
SPEAKING WITH WORDS THAT WOULD
SOONER BE ATTRIBUTED TO THE
PERSON NEAR YOU THAN YOURSELF.

IF THAT IS THE CASE WITH YOU, AND
YOU ARE AT THE POINT WHERE YOU
CAN RECOGNIZE THAT THAT IS
WHAT'S GOING ON, THERE ARE A FEW
THINGS YOU CAN DO.

ONE, KEEP YOUR HANDS IN YOUR POCKETS OR ON SOME TYPE OF ORGANIC (GROUNDED) SURFACE, IF YOU ARE EXPOSED AND TAKING ON OTHERS' ENERGY, IN A RESTAURANT FOR EXAMPLE. PLACE YOUR HANDS (THEY ARE TREMENDOUSLY RECEPTIVE, YOU SEE) ON THE WOODEN BAR, TABLE OR CHAIR, OR HOLD YOUR OWN HANDS TOGETHER IN YOUR LAP. ANOTHER GREAT TECHNIQUE IS TO SIMPLY GO AND WASH YOUR HANDS WITH WATER. THIS ACTS KIND OF LIKE AN ENERGETIC RE-SET, AS IT CLEANSES THE RECEPTORS IN THE HANDS AND GROUNDS YOU WITH THE WATER AT THE SAME TIME.

BUT YOU MUST UNDERSTAND THAT FOR SOME OF YOU, IT'S NOT THAT YOU

ARE GETTING INTERFERENCE FROM
ANOTHER ENERGY FIELD, IT'S THAT
YOU ARE OPTING IN TO A DRAMATIC
POWER-GRAB, EITHER YOUR OWN OR
SOMEONE ELSE'S, AND YOU'RE
PLAYING INTO CREATING AN
EMOTIONAL ROLLERCOASTER FOR
YOURSELF. IN THIS CASE IT'S YOUR
OWN EMOTIONAL BODY YOU ARE
FEELING.

THAT SECOND SCENARIO CAN BE A
BIT TRICKY UNTIL YOU LEARN
(THROUGH UNDERSTANDING THE
PROPER, REDUCED ROLE OF THE EGO)
THAT YOU ARE PLAYING INTO IT.

HERE'S WHAT YOU CAN DO TO
UNDERSTAND THE DIFFERENCE
BETWEEN UNWITTINGLY TAKING ON
OTHERS' ENERGY THROUGH

PROXIMITY, OR CO-CREATING A
DRAMA CYCLE:

PLAY WITH BEING SILENT IN THE
MOMENT.
IF YOU'RE TAKING ON
ENVIRONMENTAL ENERGY, YOU'LL
HAVE MORE BODILY SENSATIONS,
AND LESS COMPULSION TO
CONTRIBUTE YOUR OWN WORDS. AND
IF YOU DO SPEAK, YOU'LL NOTICE
THAT THE WORDS THAT COME OUT
DON'T SOUND LIKE YOUR OWN. THIS
IS AN INDICATOR THAT YOU ARE
TAKING ON SOMEONE ELSE'S "STUFF, "
AND YOU CAN RE-SET ACCORDINGLY
WITH WATER, ETC.

IF YOU FIND YOU CANNOT DISCIPLINE
YOURSELF TO LISTEN INSTEAD OF
SPEAK WHEN YOU ARE
EXPERIENCING AN ENERGETICALLY

CHARGED ENVIRONMENT, THIS INDICATES THAT YOU ARE BUYING IN, IN SOME WAY, TO A LOWER VIBRATIONAL EXCHANGE, AND YOU'RE GETTING A KICK BACK FROM IT, USUALLY IN THE FORM OF ATTENTION, "I'M RIGHT"-NESS, ETC.

IT'S IMPORTANT TO LEARN TO IDENTIFY THE DIFFERENCE BETWEEN THE TWO SCENARIOS BECAUSE THE FIRST ONE IS EASILY AND DISCRETELY REMEDIED, AND THE LATTER IS A PIVOT POINT OPPORTUNITY FOR YOU, WHICH CAN POINT YOU TOWARD YOUR OWN GROWTH IN AWARENESS AND THE ABILITY TO TRANSCEND FUTURE ENERGETIC MISMATCHES.

Really great stuff to play with, I think! Have a beautiful day, friends! XO, Liz

Message 11:
Are You Going Out With That Stain On Your
Shirt?

YOU MIGHT BE READY TO RETHINK
YOUR TOLERANCE FOR
INTERACTIONS THAT STAIN YOU.

A STAINING INTERACTION IS ONE
THAT SEEMS TO LEAVE AN
ENERGETIC "STAIN" ON YOU ONCE
YOU WALK AWAY FROM IT. HOURS/
DAYS/MONTHS/YEARS LATER, YOU
STILL FEEL STAINED.

WE CAN GET STAINED FROM PERFECT
STRANGERS, OR FROM PEOPLE WE'RE
IN LIFELONG RELATIONSHIPS WITH,
AND WE CAN ALSO BEAR STAINS FROM
PAST RELATIONSHIPS WITH PEOPLE
WE'RE OUT OF TOUCH WITH NOW.

MOST LIKELY, YOU'RE WALKING
AROUND WITH AT LEAST ONE OF
THESE STAINS RIGHT NOW. THEY CAN

STICK AROUND FOR A LIFETIME IF
YOU LET THEM.

IDENTIFY AN EXISTING EMOTIONAL
STAIN THAT YOU WEAR (USUALLY
FROM A PAST CONVERSATION/
RELATIONSHIP.) NOW LINE YOURSELF
UP WITH THE EMOTION OF THAT
STAIN. REMEMBER THE WORDS USED,
IF YOU CAN, OR THE ENERGY THAT
LEFT ITS MARK ON YOU.

NOW, ASK THE CURRENT ADULT YOU
TO IDENTIFY WHETHER OR NOT YOU
HAVE A BELIEF SYSTEM ABOUT
YOURSELF THAT SUPPORTS AND
MAINTAINS THAT STAIN.

IF YOU ARE LINING UP WITH THE
ENERGY THAT GENERATED THAT
STAIN AND IDENTIFYING YOURSELF
BY IT, YOU'RE EITHER USING THAT AS
A BADGE TO GET ATTENTION, OR
YOU'RE READY TO CREATE AN
OVERRIDE BUTTON AND MOVE ON

WITH YOUR LIFE, DEFINED ONLY BY YOURSELF.

OK, NOW LET'S GO BACK TO BROADEN YOUR AWARENESS AND PREVENT THESE ENERGETIC STAINS IN THE FIRST PLACE. THIS WILL BE SELF-TALK WORK. IT'S IMPERATIVE THAT, IF YOU FEEL YOU'VE BEEN PRONE TO ENERGETIC STAINS, YOU CUE UP SOME REPETITIVE SELF-TALK TRACKS THAT WILL BECOME THE "BACKGROUND MUSIC," IF YOU WILL, FOR CONVERSATIONS WHERE YOU FEEL VULNERABLE.

AND HERE'S A TIP FOR INSTANT "STAIN" REMOVAL:
QUICK BREATHS. ALMOST A SHOOSH-ING BREATH, FOCUSING ON THE EXHALE, FOR AT LEAST 5X, IN AND OUT. AS SOON AS YOU FEEL AWARE OF THE STAIN, "SHUSH" IT OUT.

That last bit sounds almost like a commercial for laundry soap, but I have to say, it's amazing to me just HOW MUCH COMES BACK TO THE BREATH. I don't know if we realize or remember what a powerful healing tool the breath is. And it's so versatile! We can tap into a slow rhythm to get us down into meditation, we can use it to manage emotions in real time, and now, from this post, I'm realizing that it even has retroactive healing powers.

I actually love the fast "shooshing" and I'm going to put it to use for sure. It almost reminds me of that full body shakedown that a dog does after a teeth-gnashing bark-fest at another dog. Almost all of us have seen a dog reset itself that way, and go happily on his merry way, completely leaving the altercation behind!

Well, since most of us can't shimmy that effusively, I think the fast breath idea is great for us.

Love you guys!
XO, Liz

Message 12:
Worth Every Minute

Question: How can we best cultivate compassion for someone we don't understand?

BE ONE WITH THE ESSENCE OF THE PERSON, WHEN YOU ARE NOT WITH THEM. THIS IS YOUR PREREQUISITE FOR FACE TO FACE CONVERSATION, ESPECIALLY IF YOU ARE FINDING IT DIFFICULT TO ACT COMPASSIONATELY WHEN YOU ARE TOGETHER. IT IS ALSO YOUR PREREQUISITE FOR TALKING ABOUT THE INDIVIDUAL WITH ANYONE ELSE.

SO, EASE INTO THIS. PRACTICE BEING WITH THEIR ESSENCE. TEMPORARILY SEPARATE THEIR ESSENCE FROM THEIR BEHAVIOR, THEIR CHARACTERISTICS, EVEN THEIR PHYSICAL APPEARANCE. JUST FOCUS ON THE ESSENCE.

NOW, TRY TO DO THE SAME FOR YOURSELF. SEE IF YOU CAN ENERGIZE YOUR ESSENCE MOST OF ALL, AND

PULL BACK THE ATTENTION AND
FOCUS YOU'VE BEEN PUTTING ON
YOUR OWN OPINIONS, BELIEFS OR
HISTORY.

SO HERE YOU ARE WITH YOUR OWN
ESSENCE, IMAGINING THE OTHER
PERSON'S ESSENCE.
DO WHAT YOU CAN TO TEMPORARILY
SUSPEND WHATEVER CONFLICT OR
EMOTIONS KEEP GETTING IN YOUR
WAY.

SET A TIMER FOR ONE MINUTE. SEE IF
YOU CAN SUSTAIN ONLY THE PURE
UNIVERSAL ENERGETIC CONNECTION
BETWEEN YOUR ESSENCE AND THE
OTHER'S ESSENCE. SPEND THAT ONE
MINUTE RELEASING THE PHYSICAL
TENSION IN YOUR BODY WHEREVER
YOU NOTICE IT.

TOMORROW, DO TWO MINUTES.

ADD JUST ONE MINUTE EACH DAY OF
THIS ESSENCE TO ESSENCE FOCUS
UNTIL YOU CAN BE WITH THIS

PERSON'S ESSENCE FOR FIVE MINUTES. KEEP USING THE TIMER, YOU REALLY NEED IT.

AT THE END OF THE FIVE DAYS, WHAT COMPASSION HAVE YOU CULTIVATED? ARE YOU READY TO SEE THE PERSON FACE TO FACE OR THINK OF THEM WITH COMPASSION? SEE IF YOU CAN CARRY THE ESSENCE CONNECTION WITH YOU.

IF NOT, GO BACK TO ONE MINUTE.

I think this is an essential tool. Not just for the people in our families or circles whom we interface with, but for people and groups we may never meet. See, it's not about absolving anyone of their poor behavior. It's about not letting their behavior CHANGE THE CHEMISTRY IN OUR OWN BODIES and destroy our inner peace!

We are responsible for the version of ourselves that leaves the house every day and goes out into the world. If we need to alchemize some bad vibes first so that we don't poison anyone else with them, we need some tools to use, so now we have one!

Sending love, guys!
XO Liz

Message 13:
What To Do When You Are Freaking Out

GO BACK INTO THE WOMB. GO BACK AND RECLAIM THE NURTURING ENVIRONMENT YOU ONCE HAD. THE WOMB WAS THE PERFECT MODEL FOR YOUR SUSTAINABILITY. YOU'RE FREAKING OUT BECAUSE YOU FEEL LIKE THAT ENVIRONMENT IS LOST. IT'S NOT LOST. BUT IT HAS BEEN FORGOTTEN.

IT'S TIME TO REMEMBER THE WOMB AND GO BACK.

GO BACK TO THE <u>SHELTER</u> OF THE WOMB...
CREATE WARMTH AND PHYSICAL COMFORT AROUND YOURSELF. THIS COULD BE HOT BATHS, SOFTER BLANKETS, WHATEVER YOU CAN MANAGE IN ORDER TO FEEL COMFORTED, SUPPORTED AND SAFE IN A TACTILE WAY.

BLOCK OUT EXTERNALS. REMEMBER, IN THE WOMB YOU WERE PROTECTED FROM OUTSIDE INFLUENCES, LOUD SOUNDS, EVEN LIGHT. RECLAIM YOUR COCOON AT LEAST ONCE A WEEK BY SHUTTING EVERYTHING DOWN AND WRAPPING YOURSELF IN COMPLETE DARKNESS AND QUIET.

NOURISH YOURSELF WITH PURE LIFE ESSENCE AND MODERATE NUTRITION. IF SOMEONE WHO LOVED YOU MORE THAN ANYTHING WAS RESPONSIBLE FOR YOUR DIETARY INTAKE, WHAT WOULD THEY FEED YOU? EAT THAT.

GO WITHIN WITHIN WITHIN. YOU CAN GET THAT SAFETY BACK, THAT SANITY.

USE THE WOMB AS YOUR TEMPLATE AND WHEN YOU CAN'T FACE THE WORLD, RETURN, METAPHORICALLY, TO THE WOMB. YOUR WOMB. THE WOMB YOU CAN

NOW TAKE RESPONSIBILITY FOR CREATING FOR YOURSELF.

Well, simply put, I need some womb therapy. I'm going to put this into practice for at least an hour on weekends, if not more often. I think there's just something so primal about this basic need for nurturing and reclaiming our safety and sustenance. We ignore these needs to our peril, and then wonder why we're feeling depressed, isolated, malnourished.

If you're at a crisis point, I'd recommend dropping everything and creating a womb for yourself as soon as possible. There is so much safety in this. Nourish yourself first, *then* you can face the world with your lifeline intact.

Wishing you love, support and tenderness today, all.
XO Liz

Message 14:
Don't Leave Home Without It

REINVEST IN SPIRIT. WHEN YOU LEAVE THAT CONNECTION OUT OF THE MIX, YOU DRAIN OUT. AND FAST.

YOU CAN RE-NAME IT WHAT YOU WANT: PRANA, CHI, FLOW, HIGHER WHATEVER-- BUT SPIRIT IS *ESSENTIAL.* MEANING, IT'S THE ESSENCE OF YOU.

Today I am sending so much love and appreciation for the essential universal flow that is each one of you. Thank you for sharing your energy with me.

XO, Liz

Message 15:
Don't Get Mad, Get Rid Of Your Stuff

WHEN YOU FIND YOURSELF IN VICTIM MODE, YOU HAVE OPTIONS YOU AREN'T SEEING.

BEGIN ON THE MATERIAL PLANE AND REMOVE THE PHYSICAL ITEMS AROUND YOU THAT HAVE OUTSTAYED THEIR USEFULNESS. WE'RE TALKING ABOUT YOUR PERSONAL ENVIRONMENT HERE-- CLOTHING, PRODUCTS, ARTIFACTS-- TAKE A VIBRATIONAL ASSESSMENT OF THESE FIXED ITEMS THAT CONTRIBUTE TO YOUR MENTAL STATE EVERY DAY.

IT IS NOT RIDICULOUS TO GO AROUND YOUR ROOM, HOME, OFFICE AND ASK OF EACH ITEM: "HOW DOES THIS MAKE ME FEEL?" AND THEN KEEP OR DISCARD THE ITEMS BASED ON THE ANSWER TO THAT QUESTION.

YES, THIS IS ABOUT THE MATERIAL STUFF. BUT THAT MATERIAL STUFF IS THERE, INFLUENCING YOU, EITHER BECAUSE YOU CHOSE IT, OR BECAUSE YOU PUT UP WITH IT.

THE MORE YOU SUPPORT YOURSELF BY SETTING UP THE INTENTIONALITY OF YOUR SURROUNDINGS SO THAT THEY ARE IN INTEGRITY WITH WHO YOU ARE, THE MORE ROOM YOU HAVE TO BREATHE YOUR AURIC FIELD OUTWARD. AND THE MORE YOU EXPAND THIS FIELD, THE FREER YOU BECOME, AND THE FREER YOU FEEL, THE MORE FREEDOM IS BEING REFLECTED BACK TO YOU IN YOUR EXPERIENCES.

HERE'S A HINT: ANGER IS THE OPPOSITE OF FREEDOM.

SO, THIS HOMEWORK IS MANDATORY.

I get it. I get it. Love you guys. XO, Liz

Message 16:
You Are The Universe

OCEANS ABOVE YOU HOST REALMS OF WATERS THAT YOU'VE CHOSEN NOT TO PERCEIVE YET. WITHIN YOUR OWN CONNECTIVE TISSUE IS AN INNER WORLD, A MICROCOSM OF THIS OUTER ONE.

USE YOUR OWN BODY AND WHAT YOU KNOW ABOUT IT TO MODEL FOR YOU WHAT YOUR OUTER, UNIVERSAL WORLD COULD BE.

LOOK AT HOW YOUR BODY FUNCTIONS AS A WHOLE, AND GO DEEPER INTO YOUR GRAND, VAST, UNIVERSAL BODY. WHAT DO YOUR UNIVERSAL ARMS EMBRACE? WHAT CAN YOU SEE WITH YOUR UNIVERSAL EYES?

INCLUDE EARTH, SKY AND INFINITY IN YOUR MODEL. GROW YOURSELF

INTO YOUR TRUE SIZE AND
EXPRESSION, WHICH EXTENDS INTO
THE VAST UNIVERSE OF ALL THAT IS.
BECAUSE THAT UNIVERSE IS YOU.

Take it in. How would your earthly experience
change if you lived from this perspective?
XO, Liz

Message 17:
The Process

AROUND THE CORNER THERE IS THIS
AWARENESS THAT WILL HELP YOU
TRANSCEND THE WEIGHT OF THE
MOMENT YOU'RE IN. IT'S CALLED
TRUST, AND THE WAY YOU GET THERE
IS HAVING FAITH IN **THE PROCESS**.

WHAT DOES THAT MEAN? THAT
MEANS THAT THERE AREN'T JUST
"STEPS" TO TAKE TO GET FROM HERE
TO THERE. IT'S ACTUALLY A SUPER-
SUBTLE, NEVER-ENDNG **PROCESS**
THAT CARRIES ON AND CARRIES ON
NO MATTER WHAT STAGE OF THE
"STEPS" YOU THINK YOU'RE DOING.

WHEN YOU MEET UP AGAINST
RESISTANCE WHEN IT COMES TO
YOUR GOALS, OR WHEN YOU FIND
YOURSELF REVISITING A STEP YOU
THOUGHT YOU'D ALREADY CROSSED
OFF YOUR LIST, IT'S BECAUSE **THE

PROCESS** IS BIGGER AND BETTER THAN THAT.

YOUR PROCESS WAS DIVINELY DESIGNED BY YOU TO BRING OUT YOUR SELF MASTERY, UNFOLDING LIKE A GORGEOUS ROSE, EACH AND EVERY DAY FOREVER.

Trust your inner process. It is so uniquely yours!
Love you all,
XO Liz

Message 18:
Time To Rearrange

REARRANGE YOUR LIFE AROUND YOUR FEARS AND YOU'LL END UP IN PAIN. REARRANGE YOUR LIFE AROUND YOUR TRUTH AND YOU'LL ACCESS THE JOYS THAT ONLY AUTHENTICITY CAN BRING.

It's a call to action. I'm in!
XO, Liz

Message 19:
You Were Once A Fearless Creature

YOU WERE ONCE A FEARLESS
CREATURE WHO NAVIGATED
THROUGH LIFE BASED ON HOW
THINGS MADE YOU FEEL. AT SOME
POINT, YOU ABANDONED THAT
NAVIGATION SYSTEM IN FAVOR OF
PLEASING OTHERS, OBLIGING
STRANGERS, AND WANTING TO BE
LIKE EVERYONE ELSE INSTEAD OF
WANTING TO BE UNIQUELY YOU.

THE ROAD BACK IS SO SIMPLE. YOU
JUST START REMOVING EVERYTHING
YOU PUT ON FOR ANYONE ELSE BUT
YOU.

START WITH YOUR HABITS, LIKE THE
WAY YOU DO OR DON'T SPEAK UP, THE
WAY YOU WORK YOUR DAY TO AVOID
AUTHENTICITY, OR THE WAY YOU
TREAT YOUR OWN BODY BY FUELING
IT WITH THOUGHTS THAT YOU DON'T

TRULY BELIEVE, OR FOOD THAT IS
SLOWLY KILLING YOU.

YOU CAN SIMPLY ASK YOURSELF, AT
ANY POINT IN YOUR DAY, "IS WHAT I'M
DOING IN THIS VERY MOMENT TRUE
TO WHO I REALLY AM?" YOU'LL GET
THE ANSWER INSTANTLY, AND ONCE
YOU DO, RUN WITH IT!

Whoosh! Fresh thoughts coming in!
XO, Liz

Message 20:
What's Your Problem?

OTHER PEOPLE NOT LIVING YOUR TRUTH?
NOT YOUR PROBLEM!

<u>YOU</u> NOT LIVING YOUR TRUTH?
BIG PROBLEM!

XO, Liz

Message 21:
We're All In The Garden

IF EVERYONE GREW UP SPIRITUALLY
AT THE SAME RATE, WE WOULDN'T
HAVE THE CONTRAST OF
EXPERIENCES TO MAKE OUR
GROWING GROUND SO FERTILE.

BE WITH YOURSELF AS YOU GROW
AND DON'T CONCERN YOURSELF
WITH THE GROWTH RATES OF
OTHERS. BE A FRIEND TO YOURSELF
AND LET THE REST OF THE FOLKS
JUST BE.

THE ONLY THING YOU CAN "TEACH"
ANYONE ISN'T EVEN SOMETHING YOU
CAN TEACH. IT'S JUST LOVING
YOURSELF.

LOVING YOURSELF AND ACTING ON
THAT LOVE WILL TEACH YOU AND
EVERYONE ELSE ALL THERE REALLY
IS TO LEARN.

Learning to do this openly was a big step for me. Being willing to love myself "out loud" as it were. But once I started, I couldn't stop. And my love for myself (and my journey) has grown so strong that it's helped me to love others so much more. Because I see myself in them, and I see them in me.

XO, Liz

Message 22:
Open Your Moment

GOING FURTHER EACH DAY MEANS
THAT EVERY TIME YOU BREATHE, THE
BREATH BEFORE IT IS GONE.

THE MOMENT IS GONE, AND YOU'RE
IN A NEW MOMENT.

IT'S A REBIRTH, AN OFFERING OF THE
SOUL, DIRECTLY FROM GOD TO
YOU. IT'S A GIFT-- THAT MOMENT. AND
THEN THE NEXT AND THE NEXT.

THE GIFTS OF MOMENTS KEEP
COMING. BUT IF YOU'RE STUCK ON
MISINTERPRETING THE GIFT FROM
15,000 MOMENTS AGO, THEN YOU LEAP
OVER THE INTERIM MOMENTS WHILE
YOU HANG OUT IN THE PAST.

GO FOR THE FLOW. MEASURE YOUR
MOMENTS BREATH BY BREATH. NOT
YEAR BY YEAR, OR SEASON BY
SEASON. THEY'RE ALL GONE. BUT THIS

GIFT, RIGHT NOW, THIS MOMENT, IS HERE. OPEN IT!

Loving you all!
XO, Liz

Message 23:
Drifting

FOR RIGHT NOW, THINK OF
HAPPINESS AS A PLACE YOU CHOOSE
TO VISIT WHEN YOUR EGO AND MIND
ARE AT REST.

WHEN YOU ARE ALIGNED, YOUR
SPIRIT KNOWS WHERE IT LIKES TO
LIVE AND IT WILL ACCESS WHATEVER
MAP IT NEEDS TO USE TO GET YOU
THERE. BUT WHEN YOU ARE OUT OF
SYNC, YOUR INNER WISDOM IS
CLOUDED BY SUPERFICIALITIES THAT
YOU'VE TEMPORARILY DECIDED TO
PRIORITIZE.

SEE IF YOU CAN LET GO TODAY, AND
DRIFT FOR A MINUTE. WHEN YOU
REMOVE THOUGHT, AND ALLOW
YOURSELF TO DRIFT, WHERE DO YOU
NATURALLY END UP, EMOTIONALLY?

IF YOU END UP FEELING "STUCK" WITHIN YOUR THOUGHTS, PAIN, EMOTIONS, ETC... WELL THEN YOU'RE NOT DRIFTING, ARE YOU?

Ohhhhhhhhhh......!
Sending love, !
XO, Liz

Message 24:
Waking Up To This Part Of Your Journey

THERE WAS A BEGINNING TO ALL OF
THIS, BUT YOU MIGHT HAVE MISSED
IT. THERE WERE CLUES, SIGNALS,
SIGNS, ALL OF THAT. BUT FOR
WHATEVER REASON YOU DIDN'T SEE
THEM, OR YOU COULDN'T SEE THEM.

BUT NOW, HERE YOU ARE, AT THIS
STAGE OF THE GAME, "SEEING
THINGS" MORE CLEARLY FOR WHAT
FEELS LIKE THE FIRST TIME! SO, FEEL
IT ALREADY! SEE WHAT'S TRYING TO
HAPPEN IN YOU!

THEN ONCE YOU ACKNOWLEDGE
THIS NEW AWARENESS, THIS "WAKING
UP" THAT YOUR SOUL IS DOING AT
THIS ABSOLUTELY PERFECT TIME, YOU
CAN HAVE FUN GOING BACK AND
RETRACING. YOU'LL BE ABLE TO SEE
THE CUES AND CLUES YOU MIGHT
HAVE BEEN TOO UNAWARE TO SEE
BACK THEN.

AND INSTEAD OF BEATING YOURSELF UP ABOUT THAT, YOU CAN STOP WITH THE OLD HABITS, KEEP THE EYES OPEN THIS TIME, AND FINALLY STEP INTO YOUR BIRTHRIGHT-- THE TRANSFORMING **YOU** THAT GETS TO WALK THESE NEXT STEPS WITH A CLEARER VIEW, A BROADER VIEW, OF WHAT IS TRYING TO COME THROUGH YOU IN THIS LIFETIME!

Congratulations!
XO, Liz

Message 25:
Don't Believe In Yourself

WHEN PEOPLE SAY THAT YOU SHOULD BELIEVE IN YOURSELF, WHAT THEY ARE REALLY TRYING TO DO IS HELP YOU TAP INTO YOUR POTENTIAL ON AN ENERGETIC AND SPIRITUAL LEVEL.

BECAUSE USUALLY, ABOUT THE TIME SOMEONE IS ADVISING YOU TO BELIEVE IN YOURSELF, YOU ARE CURRENTLY NOT IN THE STATE YOU WANT TO BE IN-- HAVING ACHIEVED SOMETHING, LOOKING OR FEELING A CERTAIN WAY, ETC. SO SOME ENCOURAGING PERSON WILL COME ALONG AND TRY TO GET YOU TO BELIEVE IN YOURSELF.

BUT IT GETS TRICKY WHEN YOU TRY TO BELIEVE IN YOURSELF, BECAUSE YOU IDENTIFY THE WORD SELF WITH WHAT YOU CAN PHYSICALLY SEE IN

FRONT OF YOU, WHICH MAY NOT BE
WHAT YOU CURRENTLY WANT.

YOU GET STUCK BECAUSE YOU FEEL
YOU HAVE NO EVIDENCE OF YOUR
POTENTIAL.

SO LET'S STOP DOING THE BELIEVE IN
YOURSELF THING, AND LET'S GO FOR
BELIEVING IN ALL THAT IS: THE
SUPREME CREATIVE POWER OF THE
UNIVERSE.

BECAUSE YOU CANNOT DENY
THAT YOU ARE THAT POWER,
INCARNATE.

AND WHEN YOU KNOW AND
UNDERSTAND THAT, YOU BELIEVE IN
IT. AND BELIEVING IN THE SUPREME
CREATIVE POWER OF THE UNIVERSE
MEANS BELIEVING IN YOU.

Step into your power today. The universe has
your back. XO, Liz

Message 26:
Are You Discriminating Against Joy?

WHEN PEOPLE BLOCK THEMSELVES
FROM RECEIVING MONEY FOR WHAT
THEY OFFER, IT'S BECAUSE THEY
HAVE PUT UP A WALL OR DISTINCTION
BETWEEN VALUING JOY AND
VALUING EFFORT.

OUR CULTURE OFTEN EXPECTS
PEOPLE WHO LOVE THEIR WORK TO
DO IT FOR FREE! "JUST FOR THE JOY
OF IT!" ARTISTS, WRITERS, MUSICIANS,
CREATORS OF ALL TYPES ARE OFTEN
UNDERVALUED AND UNDERPAID ALL
BECAUSE OF THE BACKWARD IDEA
THAT EFFORT AND JOY ARE
MUTUALLY EXCLUSIVE.

BUT ACTUALLY, WHEN SOMETHING IS
CREATED *WITH JOY* IT IS INFUSED

FOREVER WITH THAT ENERGY, WHICH
IN FACT *<u>ADDS VALUE</u>* TO THE
OFFERING.

WHEN YOU CAN PLACE VALUE
EQUALLY ON JOY AND EFFORT,
YOU'LL STOP DISCRIMINATING
AGAINST YOUR JOY ACROSS THE
BOARD. YOU'LL STOP DISCRIMINATING
AGAINST JOY IN YOUR VOCATION,
AND YOU'LL STOP DISCRIMINATING
AGAINST JOY IN YOUR DAY TO DAY
DEALINGS.

BUT IF YOU'VE SET A TONE IN ONE
ARENA (SAY, YOUR WORK) AGAINST
JOY, YOU'VE BEGUN A PRECEDENT OF
LIMITING YOUR JOY, AND THAT CAN
INFUSE THE REST OF YOUR LIFE WITH
LIMITED EXPERIENCES.

FOR EXAMPLE, ONCE YOU'VE DISCRIMINATED AGAINST JOY BEING A PART OF YOUR WORKPLACE OR SOURCE OF INCOME, YOU'LL START TO SHOW UP WITH THOUGHTS LIKE : "RELATIONSHIPS ARE HARD", "EVERYTHING WORTH DOING OR HAVING MUST BE EFFORTFUL", "IF IT'S NOT DIFFICULT, IT'S NOT WORTH DOING", ETC.

AND CAN YOU SEE HOW THAT THOUGHT PATTERN SETS YOU UP TO PINCH OFF THE FLOW OF JOY IN ALL AREAS OF YOUR LIFE?

IF YOU PINCH OFF THAT JOY WITH YOUR BELIEF, THE NEXT THING YOU KNOW YOU'VE PINCHED YOURSELF OFF FROM LOVE, FROM MONEY, FROM JOY-FILLED ORDINARY MOMENTS,

AND FROM FRIENDSHIPS THAT UPLIFT
YOU. SEE THAT?

Duly noted! Are you discriminating against joy
in your life? Are you undervaluing what you
bring to the table? How does this either-or
principle show up in your life? What areas do
you need to break open to allow more joy and
abundance to flow IN?

I'm feeling the joy today!

XO, Liz

Message 27:
What Color Do You Need Today?

NATURE OFFERS YOU A HEALING
BALM WHEN YOU ARE SUFFERING
WITH DEEP EMOTIONAL PAIN. GET
READY FOR THIS: IT'S COLOR.

TRY THIS FOR YOURSELF: THE NEXT
TIME YOU ARE FEELING CUT OPEN BY
AN EMOTIONAL WOUND-- AS SOON AS
YOU POSSIBLY CAN, FIND A NATURAL
SOURCE OF COLOR AND STARE AT IT.
FLOWERS WORK BRILLIANTLY FOR
THIS AND IF YOU THINK ABOUT IT ,
IT'S NO SECRET WHY WE GIVE AND
RECEIVE FLOWERS AROUND
EMOTIONAL OCCASIONS.

TAP INTO THE INCREDIBLE HEALING
PROPERTIES THESE FLOWERS POSSESS.
YOU WILL KNOW RIGHT AWAY WHAT

COLOR YOU ARE DRAWN TO. SEEK IT
OUT, AND TAKE TIME GIVING
YOURSELF THIS THERAPY.

SIT WITH THE FLOWER YOU CHOSE
AND TRY TO TAKE IN ALL OF THE
PROPERTIES OF ITS COLOR. THAT
COLOR HAS RESONANCE. THAT IS WHY
YOU ARE RESPONDING TO IT. DON'T
CUT OFF THE INTERACTION, STAY
WITH IT AS LONG AS YOU CAN.

IF YOU CAN OBTAIN THE FLOWER
AND BRING IT INTO YOUR SPACE
THAT'S FANTASTIC. IF NOT, GO TO
WHERE YOU CAN FIND AND SPEND
TIME WITH THE COLOR THAT YOU
ARE DRAWN TO.
IN A PARK, IN A FLOWER SHOP,
WHATEVER YOU CAN MANAGE.

YOUR EMOTIONAL BODY WILL KNOW EXACTLY WHAT COLOR IT NEEDS. BUT YOU MUST OPEN AND ALLOW THIS FREQUENCY TO INTERFACE WITH YOUR OWN. DO NOT SECOND GUESS THIS, JUST LET YOURSELF RECEIVE THE HEALING.

THINK ABOUT IT: WHY DO YOU HAVE THE IMMEASURABLE VARIETY OF SUBTLE COLORS IN NATURE? WHAT IS THEIR PURPOSE AND VALUE? WHY DO YOU GRAVITATE TOWARD CERTAIN COLORS IN CERTAIN MOMENTS? <u>IT'S BECAUSE THEY HEAL</u>. THESE COLORS ARE HERE TO HEAL. OTHERWISE THE WORLD WOULD BE BLACK AND WHITE.

These powerful healers are all around us. On purpose. Thank you, Earth, for this healing bounty. XO, Liz

Message 28:

What Lights You Up?

WHEN IS THE LAST TIME YOU FELT SO
ALIVE THAT YOU COULD ACTUALLY
FEEL THAT YOU WERE GIVING OFF
ENERGY?

IF YOU CAN IDENTIFY A RECENT
EXPERIENCE, YOU ARE ALIGNED
WITH YOUR SOURCE. YOU KNOW
WHAT TO DO TO KEEP YOUR
CHANNEL OF ENERGY WIDE OPEN
AND FLOWING, AND YOU HAVE A GO-
TO ACTIVITY THAT WILL KEEP YOU IN
THAT PLACE.

BUT IF YOU ARE STRUGGLING TO
REMEMBER ONE OF THESE
EXPERIENCES, THEN YOU'RE
STANDING AT A DISTANCE FROM
YOUR TRUE SELF, AND YOU ARE

SUFFERING FOR IT, WHETHER YOU'RE CONSCIOUSLY AWARE OF IT OR NOT.

ONE WAY YOU CAN TAP INTO YOUR INNER LIGHT AND OPEN UP YOUR CIRCUIT IS TO ASK YOURSELF:

WHAT DID I SPEND MY TIME DOING BEFORE I EVER HAD A JOB?

BY ASKING YOURSELF THIS QUESTION, YOU ARE IDENTIFYING WHAT MADE YOU FEEL ALIVE, OR "LIT UP" WITH NO AGENDA ATTACHED, WHEN THERE WAS NO COMPULSION TO MONETIZE YOUR ENDEAVORS.

WHAT DID YOU SPEND YOUR TIME DOING THAT WASN'T A "MEANS TO AN END?" CIRCLE BACK. GO STRAIGHT TO THAT ACTIVITY AND DO IT NOW. DO WHATEVER VERSION OF IT YOU CAN.

TWIRL THAT BATON AND SEE WHAT
HAPPENS.

We are so "purpose driven" now, aren't we?
Even the spiritual seekers among us feel we
have to "be on purpose!" But what if the
number ONE purpose is knowing our joy and
living it?
XO, Liz

Message 29:

Who Is Your Plus-One?

TONIGHT, BEFORE YOU GO TO BED, SET THE TABLE FOR TOMORROW'S BREAKFAST. IT DOESN'T MATTER IF YOU DON'T EAT BREAKFAST, AND IT DOESN'T MATTER IF YOU LIVE ALONE.

SET THE TABLE FOR HOWEVER MANY PEOPLE LIVE IN YOUR HOME, PLUS ONE.

THEN, GO TO SLEEP KNOWING THAT THE "TABLE IS SET" FOR YOUR PLUS-ONE TO JOIN YOU THE NEXT DAY.

IN THE MORNING WHEN YOU GET UP, YOU'LL TAKE NOTICE OF THE TABLE SETTING, AND ANY TIME YOU USE OR PASS THAT TABLE OR THINK OF IT

DURING THE DAY, LET THE QUESTION COME UP : WHO IS MY PLUS-ONE TODAY?

WHO IS WANTING TO COME INTO MY LIFE TODAY? WHO WOULD I INVITE TO SIT AT THIS CAREFULLY PREPARED PLACE AT MY TABLE, THE HEART OF MY HOME?

IS IT A FRIEND I WISH I SAW MORE OFTEN?
IS IT A DEPARTED LOVED ONE I'M READY TO CONNECT WITH ENERGETICALLY?
IS IT A PIECE OF MY OWN SELF THAT I'VE BEEN NEGLECTING?
IS IT THE PARTNER I NEVER SEE?
IS IT MY CHILD, OR MY OWN INNER CHILD?

YOU GET TO CHOOSE, EACH DAY, WHO YOU WANT TO INVITE IN TO BE A BIGGER PARTICIPANT IN YOUR LIFE. THAT GUEST CAN BE A DIFFERENT PERSON EACH DAY.

BUT KEEP SETTING ONE EXTRA PLACE AT YOUR TABLE, BECAUSE SOMEONE IS WANTING TO COME IN. SOMEONE CAN'T WAIT TO ACCEPT THAT INVITATION.

FOR A WHILE, THE EFFORT MAY BE SYMBOLIC AS YOU GLANCE AT THE PLACE SETTING EACH DAY. BUT IF YOU DO THIS, IF YOU ACTUALLY SET THIS EXTRA PLACE AT YOUR TABLE, YOU'LL BE REMINDED OF THIS SPACE EVERY DAY. EVEN WHEN YOU ARE NOT AT HOME, YOU'LL KNOW THAT THERE IS A PLACE SET AT YOUR TABLE FOR SOMEONE SPECIAL.

AND NEXT THING YOU KNOW, YOUR
WORLD WILL TAKE ON A NEW
RICHNESS, BECAUSE YOU TOOK THE
TIME TO MAKE A PLACE AT YOUR
TABLE AND IN YOUR HEART, FOR
SOMEONE WHO WANTS TO BE THERE
WITH YOU.

Sending love to you today!

XO, Liz

THERE IS A PARTICULAR SYMBOL YOU
HAVE BEEN IGNORING, AND IT'S
READY TO SHAKE YOU UP IN THE
BEST POSSIBLE WAY!

IT'S PROBABLY A NATURAL ELEMENT
(CREATURE, TYPE OF TREE, CERTAIN
SOUND) BUT IT CAN ALSO BE AN ITEM
OR IMAGE.

EITHER WAY, IT'S BEEN TRYING TO
GET YOUR ATTENTION, BECAUSE IT
HOLDS A SPECIAL MEANING FOR YOU,
CONNECTED TO A MEMORY YOU
HAVE.

YOU DON'T HAVE TO RACK YOUR
BRAIN TO FIGURE OUT WHAT IT IS,
BECAUSE IT IS CONTINUING TO SHOW
UP FOR YOU, DAY AFTER DAY, UNTIL

YOU FINALLY BRING YOUR
AWARENESS TO IT.

WATCH FOR IT, BECAUSE IT'S COMING
THROUGH TODAY. AND ONCE YOU
ACKNOWLEDGE IT, YOU'LL KNOW
WHAT IT'S THERE TO REMIND YOU OF.
AND ONCE YOU ALLOW IT TO BE A
MESSENGER, IT WILL INTRODUCE YOU
TO ALL OF THE VARIOUS
SYMBOLS THAT MAKE UP YOUR OWN
UNIQUE SOUL LANGUAGE.

AND WHEN YOU START RECOGNIZING
THAT LANGUAGE, YOU'LL WALK WITH
THE ASSURANCE OF ONE WHO HAS
CHOSEN YOUR OWN ADVENTURE,
AND WHO IS FOLLOWING THE
BEAUTIFUL TRAIL MARKERS THAT
YOU YOURSELF CREATED.

I love being the sole interpreter of my unique soul language. Some of my symbols feel sacred and secret to me, but some I can share with you. Dragonflies, certain tones, and the bird call of a red-breasted Robin are all messengers for me. What are some of yours? If you don't yet know, you will by the end of today!

Happy adventuring!

Love you!

Liz

Message 31:
New Growth

EVERY SINGLE PLANT AND FLOWER
AND BLADE OF GRASS HAS WHAT IS
CALLED "NEW GROWTH" EACH YEAR.
YOU KNOW, THE LIGHTER GREEN
CHUTES THAT BRANCH OFF OF THE
OLD GROWTH EACH SPRING.

THOSE LIVING CREATURES KEEP
CHANGING AND EXPANDING, SEASON
AFTER SEASON, BRINGING
SOMETHING NEW TO THE TABLE
EVERY YEAR.

YES, THEY MIGHT HAVE DORMANT
TIMES, WHEN THEY GO WITHIN,
RETREAT FOR THE WINTER SEASON,
SAVE THEIR RESOURCES AND SHED
THEIR OLD LEAVES, BUT WHEN THEY
RE-EMERGE, THEY DO SO BY

BRINGING NEW GROWTH TO THEIR
BEING, AND TO THE WORLD.

BUT HUMANS SEEM TO THINK THAT
THEY CAN GET TO A CERTAIN AGE
AND THAT'S IT. THEY BELIEVE "THERE
CAN'T BE MUCH MORE TO ME THAN
THIS" SO THEY CHOOSE TO IGNORE
THEIR POTENTIAL FOR NEW GROWTH.

THEN THE UNIVERSE SAYS, "OH, OK,
YOU DON'T WANT TO GROW
ANYMORE?" AND YOUR REALITY WILL
START TO REFLECT THAT DECISION
NOT TO THRIVE.

BUT HERE'S THE THING, THERE ARE
TREES ON YOUR PLANET THAT ARE
OVER 5,000 YEARS OLD, WHO HAVE
NEW GROWTH ON THEM AS WE
SPEAK.

SO, WHAT'S YOUR NEW GROWTH?

I honor the new growth wanting to spiring forth from each of us! XO, Liz

Message 32:
You Don't Have To Do Anything

YOU CAN HAVE A COMPLETELY JOY FILLED LIFE, WITHOUT HAVING ANY AGENDA AT ALL!

WHAT GETS IN YOUR WAY IS THE SENSE THAT YOU MUST BE *DOING SOMETHING* ALL OF THE TIME.

WHEN YOU RELEASE THIS COMPULSIVE *DOING*, YOU REVERT RIGHT BACK, QUITE NATURALLY, INTO YOUR OWN BEING. YOUR BEING-NESS AS IT WERE.

AND FROM THERE YOU KNOW EXACTLY WHAT TO DO BECAUSE YOU KNOW THAT YOU DON'T HAVE TO DO ANYTHING.

Hope this message finds its place right where
you need it today!

Love you!
XO Liz

Message 33:
It's Right In Front Of You

THE BIGGEST MISTAKE YOU ARE
CURRENTLY MAKING IS DISMISSING
WHAT IS LITERALLY RIGHT IN FRONT
OF YOU.

YOUR DESIRE FOR SOMETHING MORE
IMPORTANT IS OVERRIDING YOUR
RECEPTION OF THE BLATANT SIGNS
AND SYMBOLS (WHICH YOU'VE ASKED
FOR AND PLANTED YOURSELF!) THAT
YOU ARE OBSERVING RIGHT NOW.

INSTEAD OF DRIFTING AWAY FROM
WHERE YOU ARE, WHAT IF YOU TOOK
STOCK *MOMENT BY MOMENT* OF
WHAT LIES DIRECTLY IN FRONT OF
YOU, FOR THIS YOU SEE IS YOUR OWN
REFLECTION. THIS IS WHAT YOUR

SOUL IS ASKING YOU TO NOTICE AND
CONSIDER.

IT MIGHT BE A SITUATION IN FRONT
OF YOU WHICH REQUIRES YOUR HELP,
IT MIGHT BE A CRACK IN THE
SIDEWALK ASKING TO BE
INTERPRETED, BUT IT MUST BE SAID:
WHAT YOU ARE LOOKING FOR IS
LITERALLY RIGHT IN FRONT OF YOUR
FACE. AT EVERY SINGLE MOMENT.

You're not missing out. What you need is with
you now!
XO, Liz

Message 34:

Purity Of Heart

PURITY OF HEART IS WITHIN YOU
ALWAYS, WHETHER YOU FEEL IT OR
NOT. THERE'S AN INNATE PURITY
THERE, AND YOUR ACCESS POINT TO
THAT PURITY DEPENDS ON HOW
MANY LAYERS OF FEAR YOU'VE GOT
STACKED UP ON TOP OF YOU.

YOUR EXPERIENCES WILL SHOW YOU
HOW IN-TOUCH YOU CURRENTLY ARE
WITH YOUR PURE GOLDEN HEART.

IF YOU'VE GOT ENERGETIC SCAR
TISSUE BUILT UP OVER YOUR HEART,
YOU CAN INDEED REMOVE IT. START
SAFELY AND SIMPLY BY CONNECTING

WITH NATURE'S PUREST ENERGY, THE NEW GROWTH OF SPRINGTIME FLORA.

SURROUND YOURSELF WITH THIS PURITY DAILY, TREAT IT AS A PRESCRIPTION AND DON'T SKIP A DAY. THIS TREATMENT IS BOTH EXTREMELY GENTLE AND EXTREMELY POWERFUL. AND IT'S SAFE ENOUGH THAT WHEN ADMINISTERED REGULARLY, IT WILL REMOVE-- LAYER BY LAYER-- THIS SCAR TISSUE, DISSOLVING IT INTO LIGHT.

REMEMBER TO THANK THE PLANT TO KEEP THE ENERGETIC CIRCUIT COMPLETE.

Thank you, Earth, for your healing bounty!
Have a beautiful day!
XO, Liz

Message 35:

Your Body Will Tell You Why It Hurts

USE THIS TECHNIQUE:

IN A WARM TUB, SUBMERGE YOUR
BODY IN WATER, TAKE A FEW
BREATHS, AND ASK YOUR BODY TO
TAKE YOU TO THE MEMORY THAT IS
CAUSING YOUR PAIN.

THE BODY WILL SHOW YOU THROUGH
SENSATION, PAIN, OR AWARENESS,
EXACTLY WHERE IN YOUR BODY THE
LOCATION IS.

PLACE THE PALM OF ONE HAND OVER
THE AREA. BREATHE SMOOTHLY IN
AND OUT AND REASSURE YOUR
BODY THAT YOU ARE PRESENT WITH
IT, AND THAT YOU ARE HERE TO
ADMINISTER LOVING KINDNESS AND

HEALING. (ALOUD IS BEST, THE BODY CAN FEEL THE VIBRATION OF YOUR VOICE.)

AFTER YOU MAKE THIS VERBAL PROMISE, REMOVE YOUR HAND FROM THE SITE OF THIS EMOTIONAL WOUND (ALL WOUNDS ARE EMOTIONAL) AND ASK YOUR BODY TO TELL YOU THE STORY OF THAT INJURY.

LISTEN AND DON'T SECOND GUESS WHAT YOU HEAR. YOUR BODY WILL TELL YOU THE TRUTH.

ONCE YOUR BODY COMMUNICATES WITH YOU, THANK IT FOR THE INFORMATION. PLACE YOUR HAND ON YOUR BODY AGAIN AND VERBALLY REAFFIRM YOUR COMMITMENT TO HELP YOUR BODY.

THEN REMOVE YOUR HAND AND ASK THE BODY WHAT IT NEEDS TO HEAL. LISTEN AND BE READY TO HEAR YOUR BODY'S RESPONSE. BE OPEN TO ALL SORTS OF RESPONSES, FROM "I NEED YOU TO GIVE ME MORE WATER" TO "I NEED YOU TO FORGIVE YOUR MOTHER."

THE BODY KNOWS WHAT IT NEEDS. RESPECT ITS WISDOM AND HONOR ITS WISHES. THIS IS WHAT IS MEANT BY *SELF HEALING* AND, IN TRUTH, ALL HEALING MUST BE SELF HEALING, OR THE TREATMENT WILL BE INCOMPLETE.

Sending love and healing support!

XO, Liz

Message 36:
What Do You Think?

ORGANIZE YOUR THOUGHTS AROUND
YOUR DEEPEST DESIRES. MAKE A
PLAN; NOT JUST FOR WHAT YOU WANT
TO DO, BUT FOR HOW YOU WANT TO
THINK!

BY NOW YOU KNOW YOURSELF WHEN
IT COMES TO YOUR MENTAL
PATTERNS. INTERCEPT THE
THOUGHTS THAT DON'T SERVE YOU!
STOP THEM IN THEIR TRACKS,
BECAUSE THEY ARE SO POWERFUL, SO
VERY VERY POWERFUL NOW, THAT
YOU SIMPLY <u>CANNOT</u> AFFORD TO LET
THEM RUN IN ANY DIRECTION THAT
DOESN'T LINE UP WITH WHAT YOU
WANT.

Lots of you are noticing that you're at a threshold where thoughts manifest more quickly than ever, for better or for worse! This is happening for two reasons:

First, it's because the neural pathways you've been paving have been active for decades (assuming we're all adults here.) That repetition makes it hard to change unless we choose to be conscious of our thoughts.

Second, you must know that you are stepping into your power as a creative force.

We've had this power ALL ALONG, but for about a gazillion reasons this flow and force often gets squelched mid-childhood and we've got to get back to work to claim it as our creative birthright! Collectively we are poised for this shift in consciousness, and those who are tapped into their creative power are popping up all around you, just look!

Take note today of any thought that keeps repeating. Freeze that thought and take a good hard look at it. Then ask yourself these questions and write down the answers so that you can be very honest with yourself:

1. What is the thought? (Go ahead and write down the repeating thought.)

2. What is the frame of mind I'm typically in when this thought enters my mind? (Am I stressed, tired, have I eaten?)

3. Whose presence am I in (or whose presence have I been in recently) when this thought occurs to me?

4. What behavior does this thought almost always elicit in me?

5. What reaction does my behavior listed in #4 bring out from those around me?

6. Is this thought raising my vibration or lowering it? If it's lowering it, am I willing to get rid of that thought?

7. What intervention (phrase, action) will I use the next time that thought comes up?

8. If there is another person typically affected by my thought (child, partner, coworker, friend), what amends do I need to make with them because of what this thought has done to our relationship?

9. Is there an emotional payoff I receive from holding onto this thought? (attention, martyrdom, victimhood, entitlement, "rightness", false power?)

10. When I interrupt this thought, how can I show myself compassion and honor my change?

Sending love to all of you!
XO, Liz

Message 37:

How To Stop Doing That Thing That You
Can't Stop Doing

WHEN YOU'RE AT YOUR MAX, AND
YOU REPEAT PATTERNS IN SPITE OF
YOURSELF, THIS IS A CLUE THAT
THERE IS SOMETHING IN YOUR
EMOTIONAL WIRING THAT HAS NO
OVERRIDE SWITCH YET. YOU <u>WANT</u> TO
STOP OR CHANGE BUT FEEL YOU
CAN'T, IT'S LIKE YOU HONESTLY CAN'T
CONTROL YOURSELF.

KNOW THAT THE OVERRIDE CAN'T
ALWAYS HAPPEN IN THE MOMENT
WHEN YOU'RE ALREADY ENACTING
YOUR HABITUATED BEHAVIOR. IN
FACT, IT CAN BE ALMOST IMPOSSIBLE
TO BREAK THE CIRCUIT OF THAT
WIRING IN THE MOMENT THAT IT'S
AFFECTING YOU.

SO THE KEY IS TO GO INTO YOURSELF
IN THE MORNING, FIRST THING, AND
SORT YOURSELF OUT. ASK FOR HELP
WHERE YOU CAN GET IT, FROM THE
SPIRITUAL PLANE. ASK GOD, ANGELS,
GUIDES FOR HELP, AND TAKE AT
LEAST 5 MINUTES TO **GROUND**
YOURSELF DOWN DOWN DOWN OUT
OF YOUR HEAD AND INTO YOUR
HEART. FIND THE LOVE THERE AND
SIT IN IT.

STAY WITH THAT FEELING UNTIL IT
STICKS. YOU WANT TO KNOW THAT
WHEN YOU GET UP AND START YOUR
DAY, THE LOVE YOU JUST CULTIVATED
COMES WITH YOU.

THIS IS THE FOUNDATION WORK YOU
NEED TO BE DOING NOW. IT MUST BE

IN PLACE BEFORE YOU CAN EXPECT
TO SEE CHANGES.

I laughed so hard when I read the advice to
"sort yourself out!" I'm going to use that
phrase all the time now. Instead of saying "I
need a break" or "I'm going into the other
room to calm down" I'm just going to breathe
and say "I'll be right back, I'm gonna go sort
myself out." It's just exactly right.

XO, Liz

Message 38:
Living In High Vibration

WHEN YOU ARE OPERATING AT A
VERY HIGH VIBRATION, YOU WILL
KNOW IT, BECAUSE NOT ONLY WILL
YOU BE IMPERVIOUS TO INFLUENCES
THAT WOULD TYPICALLY TRIGGER
YOU, BUT YOU'LL FIND THAT YOU ARE
ACTUALLY CHANGING THE
VIBRATIONAL ENERGY OF THE
SITUATIONS YOU FIND YOURSELF IN.

THIS FREQUENCY SHIFT IS USUALLY
BROUGHT ON BY A PARTICULAR
THOUGHT PATTERN, SO WHEN YOU
CAN FEEL THAT YOU'VE SHIFTED
INTO HIGH-VIBE, TAKE NOTICE OF
WHAT THOUGHT PATTERN LIFTED
YOU TO THAT PLACE. KEEP IT UP!

I love the flow of this guidance-- I hope it's been as helpful to you as it has to me. The last few Messages are really bringing it home as far as our ability to be transforming our entire experience through thought (and therefore vibration.)

Have a fantastic day, guys!
Love, Liz XO

Message 39:

Knock Knock

HOLD ONTO YOUR HATS,
TRANSFORMATION IS AFOOT TODAY!

IT'S ABOUT <u>ALLOWING IT</u>, NOT
FORCING OR CONJURING. THE
TRANSFORMATIONAL ASPECT IS
ALREADY THERE, VIBRATING WITHIN
YOU AS IT HAS BEEN SINCE YOUR
PATH BEGAN AND NOW IT IS ABOUT
SETTING ASIDE MOMENTS TO GET
OUT OF YOUR OWN WAY!

BE WITH YOURSELF TODAY IN A STATE
OF OBSERVATION: SEE FOR YOURSELF
WHAT IS TRYING TO SHIFT AND COME
THROUGH. DON'T BLAME YOURSELF
FOR THE OBSTACLES YOU'VE
CREATED THUS FAR, JUST BREATHE

THEM AWAY-- THEY KNOW WHAT TO
DO NOW.

OPEN YOUR EYES TODAY AND
BEHOLD THIS NEW YOU. BLESS YOUR
OUTDATED HABITS AND PATTERNS,
AND LET YOUR TRANSFORMED SELF
LEAD YOU TODAY.

I'm so excited, aren't you?!
Lots of love,
Liz

Message 40:
How To Meditate

SOFTEN THE BOUNDARIES OF YOUR PHYSICAL BODY WHEN YOU SIT IN MEDITATION. SENSE INTO THE FREQUENCY OF LOVE AND ALLOW YOURSELF TO BECOME ITS MATCH.

For me, that says it all.

Have a beautiful day, friends…

XO, Liz

Message 41:
You're Already There

IT'S ALWAYS A MATTER OF
PERSPECTIVE. FROM YOUR HUMAN
POINT OF VIEW, THERE ARE
CONSTRUCTS IN PLACE THAT WOULD
HAVE YOU BELIEVING THAT YOU
CAN'T HAVE THIS OR DO THAT.

UNDERSTAND THAT <u>YOUR DESIRE</u>
<u>ITSELF IS A GLIMPSE INTO A REALITY</u>
<u>IN WHICH THAT CIRCUMSTANCE</u>
<u>ALREADY EXISTS FOR YOU.</u>

YOU GET THESE WINDOWS INTO
OTHER ASPECTS AND DIMENSIONS OF
YOUR LIFE, BUT YOU QUICKLY LABEL
THEM AS SOMETHING ELSE AND
MOVE ON! YOU SAY "OH! I HAVE AN
IDEA!" OR "OH! I'VE ALWAYS WANTED
TO..." AND FOR THAT MOMENT YOU

ARE THERE, ONE WITH THE CIRCUMSTANCE THAT YOU DESIRE.

DON'T SHORTCHANGE THE EXPERIENCE OF TAPPING IN. IT'S NOT JUST A PASSING DESIRE OR RANDOM THOUGHT! THOSE VISIONS ARE YOU CONNECTING INTO ASPECTS OF YOURSELF THAT ALREADY EXIST IN THE ENERGETIC REALM.

IT'S UP TO YOU TO ENGAGE WITH THE REALITIES YOU WANT TO EXPERIENCE, AND LET YOUR PHYSICAL FORM JUST CATCH UP TO WHERE THE ENERGY IS ALREADY IN PLACE!

Rock on, Friends!
XO Liz

Message 42:
Surf's Up, Catch (the right) Wave!

GET ON BOARD WITH YOUR LIFE AND
START SURFING!

THERE ARE CURRENTS AND WAVES
AROUND YOU THAT WILL LITERALLY
FAST-TRACK YOU IN THE DIRECTION
YOU WANT TO GO.

THE VARIABLES ARE:
1. WHICH BOARD YOU CHOOSE
2. WHICH WAVE YOU CHOOSE

SENSE INTO IT. IF THE CHOICE MAKES
YOU FEEL GIDDY, ALIVE, SENSORIAL,
OR DEEP-ROOTED, YOU'VE MADE THE
RIGHT ONE!

I am so "on board" with this.

"Right choices" are indeed available to us, and the more dialed into our true selves we are, the more frequently we make those right choices.

As far as choosing the right board, what does your current "equipment" look like? Whom do you surround yourself with? What information and thoughts do you allow into your mind? How do you treat your physical body? All of these things form the composite layers of our ideal Super-Surfboards.

And as far as the waves go, think of them as flows of energy, ranging from completely defeating to utterly fulfilling. Which ones have you chosen to ride lately? How have those choices turned out for you? Are you trying to jump onto waves just because they're the ones that come in? Or are you keenly surveying the horizon for the quality of wave that's in line with the quality of the ride you want to have?

Get discerning, guys. Tune up your preferences and act on them every chance you get. Create that perfect board with your choices, and call in that perfect wave with your focused thoughts.

Then, hang loose and watch your life become YOUR life.

Love to you, good people!
XO Liz

Message 43:
Intuition Won't Help You If You Don't Act On It

TRUST THAT THING THAT JUST HAPPENED. THAT PULL, THAT PAUSE, THAT IMPULSE.

TODAY, WHEN THOSE SENSATIONS COME THROUGH, HONOR THEM <u>IMMEDIATELY</u>.

FINE TUNE YOUR INTUITIVE ABILITIES BY SHOWING UP <u>IN TANDEM WITH</u> YOUR INTUITION, ARM IN ARM, AND DEMONSTRATING THAT YOU'RE LISTENING.

YOU DO THIS BY ACTING <u>RIGHT AWAY</u> ON YOUR INTUITIVE HITS.

NO WAITING. TODAY, DO IT FOR THE ENTIRE DAY.

--YOU SENSE THAT YOU'RE SUPPOSED TO REACH OUT TO SOMEONE? CALL THEM NOW. THEY PROBABLY HAVE A MESSAGE FOR YOU OR VICE VERSA.

--YOU'RE WALKING YOUR NORMAL ROUTE AND FEEL PULLED A DIFFERENT DIRECTION? CHANGE YOUR ROUTE ON THE SPOT. YOU ARE BEING GUIDED TO AN OPPORTUNITY OR AWAY FROM HARM.

--YOU GET AN IDEA THAT ENERGIZES YOU JUST THINKING ABOUT IT? STOP THINKING ABOUT IT AND TAKE AN IMMEDIATE ACTION STEP INSTEAD. YOU HAVE NOTHING TO LOSE BUT DECADES OF STAGNANT ENERGY, SO GO!

Wishing you all a dynamic and beautiful day!
Sending love to each of you!
XO Liz

Message 44:
Low Vibrational Energy and How To Spot It

SO YOU'RE GOING ABOUT YOUR DAY
AND SUDDENLY YOU EXHIBIT A
BEHAVIOR THAT SEEMS
DISPROPORTIONATE TO THE
CIRCUMSTANCE AT HAND. YOU MAY
HAVE STEPPED INTO A POCKET OF
ENERGY THAT DOESN'T RELATE TO
YOU.

THIS CAN HAPPEN IN A PLACE OF
HISTORICAL SIGNIFICANCE OR IT CAN
BE A TAP-IN TO SOMEONE ELSE'S
ENERGY FIELD WHO IS EITHER
NEARBY OR WHO HAS LEFT A
RESIDUAL ENERGETIC IMPRINT IN
YOUR LOCATION.

WORK ON NOTICING THE ENERGY
YOU ARE WALKING INTO. AS YOU

BECOME AWARE OF IT, YOU WILL ALSO
LEARN TO MOVE WITH THE FLOW OF
THE ENERGY YOU CURRENTLY CARRY.

STEP OUT OF STEP WITH YOURSELF TO
HOP BACK INTO THE VIBRATIONAL
CURRENT YOU WANT TO RIDE.

COME TO THINK OF IT YOU MIGHT
WANT TO CHECK YOUR SYNAPSES.
YOU MIGHT BE CORRELATING AN
IMPULSE WITH A MEMORY RIGHT AT
THAT MOMENT, WHICH CAN CREATE
AN ENERGETIC DROP, THUD OR BOMB
SEEMINGLY OUT OF NOWHERE.

WHAT IF YOU COULD SEE THE FIELD?
IT WOULD MAKE SO MUCH MORE
SENSE! WELL, YOU'RE GETTING
THERE. SOMETIMES YOU WILL BE
ABLE TO SEE THE FIELD BETTER
THAN OTHERS, BUT WHAT IS

IMPORTANT IS THAT WHEN YOU SENSE IT, YOU CATAPULT THAT ENERGY OUT OF YOURSELF OR CATAPULT YOURSELF OUT OF THAT ENERGY.

I'm grateful for this message because it reminds me to be intentional about my own energy field.

Also, in case you're wondering about the advice to "step out of step with yourself..." that is actually a physical technique you can do. It has worked for me numerous times, especially in crowded environments like airports or midtown Manhattan. I've also used it when I'm driving a car.

It goes like this... When you can tell that you keep getting "stopped up" in the flow of pedestrians... you can't seem to create a fluid path through, etc... (a clue that the energy is off is if you really start to get irritated about it.)

When this happens, pull over. Literally. Whether you are on foot, or in a vehicle. Pull yourself over and out of the crowd, just for a second, then re-start.

This has worked wonders for me, and you'll see/learn right away that you were out of your flow. You had stepped (walked, driven) into energy fields that were not in alignment with yours and until you fixed it there would be nothing but stops and starts.

So, If I'm walking, I just step myself over to the side of the sidewalk, wait a second or two, then resume (in a new flow, you'll see!) If I'm driving in a neighborhood, I'll pull over to the curb, stop, and then start again. If I'm on the highway and the flow is a disjointed mess, I'll pull over to the slow lane, slow to a pace that is safe but slow enough for a bunch of cars to pass me, then I re-enter the game.

Ahhhh. Energy really is everything.

Have a great day, guys!
Sending love,
XO Liz

Message 45:
This Is Why You're So Tired

 IF YOU'RE EXHAUSTED AND YOU
TRULY CAN'T FIGURE OUT WHY, OR IF
YOU KNOW WHY BUT YOU DON'T
THINK YOU CAN DO SOMETHING
ABOUT IT, JUST ASK YOURSELF THIS
QUESTION:

"WHAT AM I PUSHING AGAINST, AND
WHAT IS IT COSTING ME?"

IF YOU WENT WITH THE FLOW
MINUTE BY MINUTE BY
MINUTE, YOU'D SEE THAT THAT
MINUTE, AND CHOOSING TO FLOW
WITHIN IT, IS ALL THERE IS, AND ALL
THERE IS TO DO!

We're being asked to weigh our choices. Not just the biggies, but the smallies.

Have you ever felt so immersed in a joyful, soul-fulfilling experience that you didn't need to sleep or eat? This happens to me when I create. When I'm in the process of creating art or music, it doesn't even OCCUR to me to take breaks or eat or rest or pee.

And that is because when I (we) tap into my (our) creativity, we are not longer relying on calories from food to sustain and energize us. We are tapping into Prana, Chi, Life Force, Creative Energy, and we are quite literally supported and sustained by that energetic flow. This is because we are practicing the rare activity of being fully present with our activity. When we do this, we have created an unimpeded flow of Prana.

But almost every other "unaware" thing we are doing is blocking that flow. So, we start drinking coffee and needing a big meal and then a snack and another snack and then some more caffeine blah blah blah.

And we get tired. So very tired. And no meal or snack or Red Bull is going to change that.

When we look honestly at our lives and what activities, relationships, or environments constantly take us OUT of our flow, we can begin to save ourselves. Because almost nothing is more important than staying in the flow.

Staying in the flow means we can be our true selves instead of a burned out, frazzled, on-edge version of ourselves. Staying in the flow means that we can bring our presence to the situation at hand, even if it's a difficult one, and be of assistance, because we aren't stepping out of flow and demanding that everything and everyone fulfills our expectations all the time.

Your vitality isn't going to come back to you because of your afternoon latte. It's going to come when you choose to pursue, every chance you get, the situations and ways of seeing that keep you fully connected to your pranic flow.

What's one shift you could try today? How about a two-parter? What if you identify one depleting habit that just needs to go and release it, and then also identify one activity that you KNOW puts you into your flow and DO IT, even if only for five minutes. Draw, meditate, call your best friend, sit in Nature, watch a slideshow of your favorite places... you get the idea.

I don't know a single person who hasn't had at least one experience where they got completely lost in their flow and felt completely energized and unstoppable. We owe it to ourselves (and to everyone in our immediate vicinity) to tap into it every chance we get.

Stay in the flow yo.
Love you guys,
XO Liz

Message 46:

I Know You From Somewhere

WHEN YOU MEET SOMEONE NEW
AND FEEL AN INSTANT WAVE OF
RECOGNITION, WHAT'S GOING ON
THERE IS THAT THEY ARE REVEALING
THEMSELVES TO YOU AS ONE OF
YOUR SOUL'S "GUIDEPOSTS" AT
PRECISELY THE RIGHT TIME IN YOUR
LIFE-- JUST AS THEY HAVE DONE FOR
YOU BEFORE IN PREVIOUS LIFETIMES.

THINK ABOUT THE PEOPLE YOU'VE
MET THROUGHOUT YOUR LIFE
WHERE YOU HAD THAT INSTANT
FAMILIARITY, REMEMBER THE
RESONANCE YOU HAD WITH THEM IN
THAT MOMENT, AND YOU'LL REALIZE
AT LAST WHAT THAT WAS ALL ABOUT!

I'm really enjoying letting this one sink in.

It's so beautiful when this phenomenon occurs, with all its giddy crackling energy. And having this explanation around these powerful pop-up relationships puts it all into perfect perspective.

Be on the lookout for these human guideposts... they're all around us if we're brave enough not to pass them by!

I love you!
XO Liz

Message 47:
Recipe For A Healing

THINK BACK TO WHEN YOU WERE A YOUNG CHILD AND RECALL WHAT REALLY MADE YOU TICK. TAKE OUT A PEN AND PAPER AND PHYSICALLY WRITE DOWN THE ANSWERS TO THE FOLLOWING QUESTIONS:

WHAT PLAY ACTIVITIES DID YOU GET LOST IN?
IN WHOSE COMPANY DID YOU FEEL THE SAFEST?
WHO LET YOU BE YOURSELF?
WHO NURTURED YOU WITH AFFECTION?
WHO NURTURED YOU WITH COMFORTING FOODS?
WHAT FOODS WERE THOSE?
WHAT SONG DID YOU PLAY ON REPEAT?

WHERE WAS YOUR FAVORITE
HIDEOUT?
WHAT DID YOU LOVE TO READ?
WHOM DID YOU SHARE YOUR DREAMS
WITH?
WHOM DID YOU CONFIDE IN?
WITH WHOM DID YOU LAUGH
LONGEST AND HARDEST?

RECIPE FOR A HEALING:
AFTER YOU ANSWER ALL OF THE
QUESTIONS ABOVE, CREATE A DAY
FOR YOURSELF WHICH INCLUDES AS
MANY OF THE PEOPLE AND
ACTIVITIES YOU LISTED AS POSSIBLE.
REALLY PACK A DAY
FILLED WITH THEM.

IF YOUR CHILDHOOD COMPANIONS
ARE NO LONGER NEAR YOU, CALL
THEM UP. IF THEY HAVE PASSED INTO

THE SPIRIT REALM, ASK THEM TO
COME CLOSE.

GIVE YOURSELF A DAY TO BE
TOTALLY IMMERSED IN RECALLING
AND RECLAIMING WHAT BROUGHT
YOU SO MUCH FULFILLMENT AS A
CHILD. AT THE END OF THAT DAY, ASK
YOURSELF WHICH OF THOSE
ELEMENTS YOU WANT TO MAKE A
POINT TO INCLUDE IN YOUR DAY TO
DAY LIFE GOING FORWARD.
REARRANGE YOUR LIFE
ACCORDINGLY.

I would really, truly encourage you to reserve a
date on your calendar for this, block it out, and
go fully into this exercise. Don't just sit at your
computer for a wistful five minutes and return
to the status quo. There is more power in this
than we can know until we actually take this

action and learn to REMEMBER ourselves again!

Sending love, guys!

XO, Liz

Message 48:

More Than Words

THERE ARE TIMES TO CHANNEL THE
ENERGY THROUGH WORDS, AND
THERE ARE TIMES TO COUNT ON
YOUR OWN UNIQUE ENERGETIC
PRESENCE IN ORDER TO SUPPORT
THE MOMENT.

WHEN YOU UNDERSTAND AND TRUST
THIS DIFFERENCE, YOU'LL KNOW JUST
WHAT TO DO, AND HOW TO SERVE
WITH LOVE, NO MATTER WHAT.

Loving all of you today... I transcribed this
Message as I was experiencing the phases of
grief that come with releasing attachment to
the human presence of an incredibly close

friend who transitioned. So when this came through, it felt like a deep sigh.

A sigh of relief that, although I use words, I don't have to use them until I'm ready, and a sigh of gratitude for the dear friends whose comforting care around my loss was sometimes eloquent, sometimes wordless, and completely present either way.

Liz

Message 49:

Making The Connection

ON YOUR OWN YOU CAN SEE ONLY SO FAR. WHAT ARE YOU WAITING FOR TO CONNECT WITH OTHERS? WHAT IS THAT THING YOU THINK YOU'LL LOSE IF YOU REACH OUT? BUY THEM THAT DRINK. SING THE SONG TO THEIR ANSWERING MACHINE. 'TIS THE SEASON TO GIVE IN TO THE CALLING OF YOUR HEART, THOSE PULSES THAT BEAT AND BEAT AND BEAT FOR LOVE. LET THEM HAVE THEIR DAY. LET THEM FIND A FRIEND.

One of my best friends and I were chatting the other day. We both spent decades of our lives as theater actresses, and we were discussing the "built in social life" that our Broadway shows in New York had provided us with.

Both of us did years of national touring as well, and my friend laughed as she exclaimed: "Being on tour is like having a mom! They make your schedule for you, they feed you, they set up your transportation, they give you spending money, tell you what time to be ready for the shuttle... all you have to do is show up!"

One other effect of the actor's life is the zero-effort social life. Theater builds really close personal connections, and those personal connections are there waiting for you at the theater every night. During my years on Broadway in New York, I'd spend my days entirely alone, making no effort to connect with friends. Why would I? I didn't need to because all of us would be at the theater by 7 p.m. and we'd have a fantastic time together and usually afterward!

I'm not denying that indeed some of my dearest friends in my life are people I met through the shows I did. I'm not saying these weren't real friendships, I'm just saying I never had to reach out to them with any effort, because every night, well, there they were!

Naturally this rhythm has its pitfalls. Namely, every show eventually closes. And in those intermittent weeks/months/years between shows, the built-in social calendar disappears. I have friends still performing today who fall apart during those unemployed phases. And it's not just because they need another job, it's because they need their friends and that interaction. And now they have to work for it.

Even though this phenomenon is acute in show business, I'll bet everybody has some aspects of their social lives that are there by default: "Oh these are my Mom friends from my daughter's preschool" or "Oh these are the guys from my office for the past 15 years"... and I'm not saying that there aren't some truly connected friendships in there, but in the name of really nurturing our lives and growth with Soul-level friendships, it might not hurt to ask ourselves... are these my real friends?

We'll get one of two answers.

If the answer is no, what would it look like to step out of default mode and make your friends on purpose instead of because you're on the same committee? I'm not minimizing this task... figuring out WHERE to go to meet your people can take some head scratching.

And if the answer is yes, when's the last time you stepped out with your friend, beyond the confines of that PTA meeting, to show her that your friendship is really meaningful to you, and has value independent of your participation in your common group?

I'll never forget the wise words spoken by a teacher of mine a few years ago, "You can't become who you really are all by yourself."

Something to think about, something to think about...

Sending love, my friends--
XO, Liz

Message 50:

It's Not Political, It's Personal

What guidance can you share around the theme of political volatility?

LET THE PEOPLE KNOW ABOUT THE FACE THEY SHOW AROUND POLITICAL ISSUES. THE BUY-IN IS ON THE MATERIAL PLANE. THE FEAR IS ON THE MATERIAL PLANE. WHEN THE FEAR BECOMES TOO MUCH, INTERFERES WITH ONE'S BASELINE HAPPINESS, THERE IS NO PROGRESS IN THE MATERIAL PLANE. YOU WON'T SEE THE PROGRESS YOU DESIRE ON THAT LEVEL WITH FEAR AS A MOTIVATOR.

What can they do?

SPEAK WITH CHILDREN IS ONE THING.
THE CHILDREN'S WISDOM IS
SIMULTANEOUSLY UNIVERSAL AND IN
THE HERE AND NOW. WHEN YOU
BRING YOURSELF INTO
CONVERSATION WITH A CHILD, DO SO
WITH THE UTMOST REVERENCE AND
RESPECT, FOR THEY ARE NOT MERELY
A LESS EXPERIENCED "YOU." THEY
ARE HIGHER MINDED, AND
NATURALLY TUNED IN, ESPECIALLY IF
THEY ARE SURROUNDED BY
RESPECTFUL PARENTS AND ADULTS.

ASK A CHILD TO TELL YOU THEIR
STORY. THAT WILL BE A HEALING
BALM FOR YOU. IF YOU FEEL YOU
DON'T HAVE ACCESS TO CHILDREN IN
YOUR LIFE, THAT IS PROBABLY A
GOOD INDICATOR THAT YOU
HAVEN'T RESPECTED THEM AS YOU
WOULD ANOTHER ADULT. IF YOU ARE

OPEN TO THAT HAVING BEEN THE CASE, YOU CAN SHIFT THAT TODAY. AND WHEN YOU DO, YOU'LL REALIZE THAT CHILDREN ARE ALL AROUND YOU. AND BIGGER STILL YOU'LL DISCOVER THAT YOU ARE STILL ONE OF THEM.

WHEN "THE WORLD" MAKES YOU WANT TO SQUEEZE YOUR EYES TIGHTLY SHUT FOREVER, SPEAK WITH A CHILD. THIS WILL HEAL YOU. BECAUSE, SOMEHOW, CHILDREN KEEP THEIR EYES OPEN. WIDE OPEN. AND YOU KNOW WHAT? THEIR HEARTS FOLLOW SUIT!

ASK THEM TO TEACH YOU WHAT THEY KNOW, NOT THE OTHER WAY AROUND. THIS IS WHAT NAMASTE IS ALL ABOUT.

Message 51:
How To Connect With "Departed" Loved Ones

TO GO TO THE "OTHER SIDE" REALLY IS NOT SO FAR. IT'S DIFFICULT FOR FOLKS TO UNDERSTAND THE SPIRIT WORLD BECAUSE THEY ARE DRAWING SUCH A CLEAR DISTINCTION BETWEEN THE PHYSICAL AND SPIRIT.

BUT THE "ONENESS" YOU EXPERIENCE AMONG THE PHYSICALLY LIVING IS ALSO RIGHT THERE WITH THE SPIRIT WORLD. YES. YOU ARE ONE WITH THE SPIRIT WORLD AS WELL. RIGHT NOW, HERE, AS YOU ARE LIVING ON EARTH.

SO MANY PEOPLE HAVE FELT... INCOMPLETE IS THE WORD THEY USE. AND THIS SENSE OF EMPTINESS ISN'T

ABOUT LACK OF CONNECTION IN THE
PHYSICAL WORLD, IT'S BECAUSE
THERE IS THIS PERCEIVED BARRIER
BETWEEN PHYSICAL AND
NONPHYSICAL.

SO YOU SEE THERE IS A PERSPECTIVE
SHIFT THERE THAT WOULD HELP SO
MANY PEOPLE WHO FEEL ALONE OR
ISOLATED. THEY SHOULD KNOW THAT
THEY ARE CONSTANTLY
SURROUNDED BY LOVING BEINGS.

IF PEOPLE WANT TOOLS TO HELP
THEM CONNECT WITH THEIR LOVED
ONES WHO HAVE PASSED... THE
PLACES THEY LOVED ARE A
BEAUTIFUL START:

NOT SO MUCH THE PLACES THEY
LIVED OR SPENT MOST OF THEIR
TIME. BUT IF THERE WERE LOCATIONS

THAT THEY WERE DRAWN TO AND
ADORED, UNDERSTAND THAT THEY
WOULD HAVE BEEN, IN THEIR
PHYSICAL LIVES, AT A HIGHER
VIBRATION WHEN THEY WERE AT
THOSE PLACES AND THEREFORE
THEY WOULD HAVE LEFT A
STRONGER VIBRATIONAL FOOTPRINT,
IF YOU WILL, AT THOSE LOCATIONS.

IF YOU CAN'T GET TO ONE OF
THOSE LOCATIONS, YOU CAN BRING
THE IMAGES OF THE PLACE INTO
YOUR HOME THROUGH PHOTOS,
PAINTINGS, EVEN AN INTERNET
SEARCH, OR EVEN BRING IMAGES OF
THAT PLACE INTO YOUR MIND'S EYE
AND USE THEM AS AN ENTRY POINT.

YOU CAN MEDITATE WITH THE
LOCATION IMAGES IF YOU CHOOSE,
BUT SOMETIMES THAT CAN INHIBIT

YOUR MEDITATION AND IT BECOMES
SOMETHING ELSE.... MORE OF A
MANTRA OR TOO MUCH
EXPECTATION. INSTEAD, JUST BRING
THE IMAGES, MENTAL AND PHYSICAL,
AROUND YOU. GET THEM INTO YOUR
DAILY ENVIRONMENT AND LET THEM
MAKE THEIR WAY INTO YOUR
PERSONAL FABRIC. THIS IS WHEN
YOU'LL BECOME RELAXED ENOUGH
TO UNDERSTAND THAT IT'S A VERY
BLURRY LINE BETWEEN WHO YOU
THINK IS HERE (WITH YOU) AND
WHO YOU THINK IS NOT.

REMEMBER, YOU ARE AS MUCH "ONE
WITH" THE SPIRIT WORLD AT ALL
TIMES AS YOU ARE WITH THE
PHYSICAL. SEE?

Sending so much love to you today. XO, Liz

Message 52:
A Walk vs A Step

YOU ARE EXPERIENCING A
PROTRACTED VERSION OF
SOMETHING YOU ARE AVERSE TO, TO
SYNCHRONIZE YOUR SYSTEM WITH
THE FLOW OF THE NOW, AND YOU'RE
"REWARDING" YOUR MENTAL SELF
WITH THE ACCEPTANCE OF THIS
PERCEPTION AS FACT.

BUT HEAVEN'S BLESSINGS INDICATE A
FREE THOUGHT PATTERN THAT
CREATES LIFETIMES. OVER AND
ABOVE YOUR CURRENT LEVEL OF
UNDERSTANDING LIES A FIELD OF
POSSIBILITY AND WONDER THAT YOU
ACCESS ONLY WHEN YOU CAN ESCAPE
YOUR CURRENT REALITY OF TIME,
WHICH FOR MOST OF YOU IS

EXCLUSIVELY DURING YOUR DREAM
STATE.

YOU CAN DELIBERATELY TUNE IN TO
YOUR DREAM STATE IF YOU WANT TO
STAY OPEN TO THE POTENTIALITIES
OF NONLINEAR TIME. YOU NEEDN'T
BE AFRAID OF IT. IT'S MERELY, LIKE
EVERYTHING ELSE, A MATTER OF
WHERE YOU CHOOSE TO PLACE YOUR
AWARENESS.

I asked for more info here...

LET'S SAY YOU DECIDE TO
UNDERTAKE A TRIP OR A PROJECT
AND YOU PRESUME IT WILL TAKE A
CERTAIN INCREMENT OF TIME TO
COMPLETE IT, YET YOU LEARN THAT
OTHERS IN YOUR CIRCLE SEEM TO
HAVE ACHIEVED SIMILAR GOALS IN
HALF AS MUCH TIME. SUDDENLY,

WITH THIS PROOF OF OTHERS' EXPERIENCES, YOU DETERMINE THAT YOUR ENDEAVOR COULD BE ACCOMPLISHED IN FAR LESS "TIME" THAN YOU INITIALLY BELIEVED.

GO OUTSIDE OF YOUR MIND NOW, AND ENVISION A SPIRAL UPON WHICH AN EVENT/JOURNEY CAN TAKE EITHER THE TIME/DISTANCE THAT IT TAKES TO GO AROUND THE CURVE OF THE SPIRAL AND UP TO THE DESTINATION ON THE NEXT RUNG/ RING OF THE SPIRAL, OR THE TRIP CAN TAKE MERELY THE TIME/ DISTANCE IT TAKES TO STEP FROM YOUR CURRENT LOCATION ON THE SPIRAL TO THE DESTINATION UP ON THE NEXT RUNG FROM YOU. LIKE, A TAKING A WALK VS TAKING A STEP.

SO, WHEN WE PERCEIVE THE ACCELERATION OR DECELERATION OF TIME, WE ARE REALLY EXPERIENCING A MOMENT (OR MORE) OF DEDICATED AWARENESS TO THAT MOMENT OR CONVERSELY WE WOULD EXPERIENCE A DEDICATED SHIFT OF OUR AWARENESS AWAY FROM THE PERCEIVED REALITY OF THAT MOMENT.

A WALK VS A STEP.

Ok. I'll admit I almost needed to start drinking coffee again when I read this.

But, there is such beauty in it, such elegance I think-- that I have to really sit with this and give it its due. And the questions this elicits walk a fine line between blowing my mind and creating waves of calm understanding.

For some back story, I'll let you know that I received this message in response to questions I was writing about this prolonged sickness I and my family had been experiencing. I got to the point one day, after my son had an onset of new symptoms, that I sort of threw up my hands into my journal, asking "What's the deal?!"

Instantly I got the message we read above.

So, the questions:

Is it really all about "what we resist persisting?"
Is our experience sincerely reflective of where we choose to place our attention?
Can we therefore deliberately create our reality, or even change it in the moment?
Would this require that we don't do a mental "override" of this concept though?
How far can we/will we go in playing with this?
What if we've never given enough credence to our dreams?

All of the questions point me toward avenues of thought I've employed before, but this new description is definitely more on the quantum level.

For example, I have absolutely created/avoided circumstances before in my life by being extremely deliberate about where I would allow my thoughts to flow, and where I wouldn't. But I wonder now if there were some self-imposed limitations, a statute of limitations I implemented, as a safety, in order to not disappoint myself or prove the theory of "where attention goes, energy flows" untrue.

What if we could go so much further as deliberate co-creators of our realities?
And how would doing so affect the collective?
From the sounds of this message, engaging with the dream state seems to be the first step.

Who's in?

Exhaling and sending love.
XO, Liz

Acknowledgements

Throughout the writing of this book, and the process that preceded it, a small but mighty group of true blue friends appeared to hold my hands and lend their ears and let me know that these messages needed to reach the world.

Some of them are long time soul companions with whom I've shared decades of life experiences. Others are new and special friends whom my soul called in at precisely the right time to bring their love, beauty and wisdom into my life.

One thing that these special people all have in common is that they are all what I call "zero-entry" friendships, meaning— they arrived on the scene so seamlessly woven into the tapestry of my soul's journey, I really can't remember them ever *not* being in my life. It's as though we've been together since the beginning of time, and indeed, perhaps we have.

These women are the sisters of my heart, mind, and soul. *Carolyn Gretta, Jessica Perrizo, Marcella Robertson, and Christine Waters,* I am forever, forever grateful.

About the Author

I'm Liz. I'm a creative artist, a partner, a mother and friend. I live in New Jersey, just outside of New York City.

As a child I spent most of my years in Boulder, Colorado, growing up in the foothills of the Rocky Mountains. Connecting with nature was so easy there, and riding or walking alone for hours and hours through the trails and bikeways was all part of growing up in the West in the '80s.

It was in Boulder that my performing career began. Ballet Arts Boulder was my home away from home, and my first professional acting job was in the Boulder Dinner Theater's production of *The Sound Of Music* at age 11.

From that point on I never stopped performing and creating: writing, acting, playing a variety of musical instruments, dancing. All of this kept me on my inevitable path to my Broadway career in New York City, where I lived for seven years before moving to New Jersey to reclaim my outdoorsy life.

I now spend my time blissfully integrating the aspects of my life that keep me fulfilled and in the flow: creating art, acting, singing and playing music (professionally and for fun), traveling as much as possible and spending time immersed in the Watchung mountain trails near my home.

My greatest joy, though, is homeschooling my young son and bearing witness to his own unique soul expressions and great wisdom. My most rapid and expansive growth has definitely taken place since becoming a mother.

Thank you for taking an interest in me and my book. I hope you'll share it with anyone you think might enjoy it. This book taught me so much about what inspiration truly is, and how nothing creative that comes through us is purely from our conscious self. The Universe is pouring the Great Creation through us, in myriad ways, each and every moment. To see this for ourselves, all we need to do is allow its glorious flow.

I wish you all love, adventure and discovery.

XO, Liz

Made in the USA
Lexington, KY
09 October 2018